Roads to Power
in Latin America

Roads to Power
in Latin America

LUIS MERCIER VEGA

Translated by ROBERT ROWLAND

FREDERICK A. PRAEGER, *Publishers*
New York · Washington · London

Frederick A. Praeger, Publishers
111 Fourth Avenue, New York, N.Y. 10003, U.S.A.
5 Cromwell Place, London, S.W.7, England

Published in the United States of America in 1969
by Frederick A. Praeger, Inc., Publishers

ENGLISH TRANSLATION © 1969 IN LONDON, ENGLAND, BY
PALL MALL PRESS

Originally published by Editions Universitaires, Paris, as
Mécanismes du Pouvoir en Amérique latine

LIBRARY OF CONGRESS CATALOG CARD NUMBER: 68-9732

Printed in Great Britain

Contents

Contents

1. Political map of Central and South America

2. Physical map of Central and South America

Introduction

High on the Bolivian plateau, beside the straight highway that connects La Paz and Lake Titicaca, the market brings together for a day a few score Indian women, young and old, with terracotta cheeks and resplendent white teeth. Spread out in front of them on a piece of paper are little heaps of dehydrated potatoes, dried fruit, bananas, manioc flour, coca leaves and medicinal herbs. Barter is the rule among these tillers of the dry windy soil; cans of alcohol are bought and carried away by the men, but apart from these the goods that change hands are mostly the produce of individuals or families. Little money circulates between buyer and seller, and the market depends less on the towns than on the long journeys—by relays of porters or on the llama's back—that link the *altiplano* with the tropical regions.

Some 1,500 miles away are the tall skyscrapers and sprawling factories of São Paulo, an industrial city that influences international markets and reacts to their fluctuations. Its varied population of 4 million includes Scandinavians and Negroes, descendants of Portuguese and Germans, thousands of Italians and every conceivable combination of races.

These are only two of the many hundreds of equally disparate faces of 'Latin' America, faces belonging to different countries, races and civilisations. Nor need one travel far to encounter such contrasts. A change of district in the same city or a short journey from the centre to the outskirts can frequently take one into an entirely different world. In Quito the Indian—a beast of burden gazing fixedly at the ground—mingles with the white man, master of the country where he is a perpetual exile. The invisible walls made up of different centuries and different memories, reinforced by a double fear, are slow to crumble. In Bahia the fisherman preserves his African skills and songs while palatial banks of concrete and marble affirm the presence of the modern world.

This superimposition of worlds and this amalgamation and fragmentation of cultures throw doubt on the meaning of the term 'Latin' America. A European's vocabulary cannot cope with so many different varieties of men, plants, trees, fruit, objects and situations. His experience is too restricted, his techniques of observation fail, and his words cannot convey what he tries to describe. He is led, inevitably, to philosophise, to simplify, or as the Spanish put it, *tocar guitarra*, to fill the empty boxes of his ignorance with empty words.

And yet there *are* societies and states in this continent, with their accompanying structures, mechanisms and forms of power. Our task, then, is to classify them and describe them, to find what is characteristic in them despite the difficulties of keeping close to facts that fit uneasily into theoretical frameworks and which defy research techniques whose conception and development were influenced by other problems.

It is probably correct to say that there exists a residual Latin America—that of the pre-Columbian civilisations—and an imported one. But this can only be a point of departure. In addition, the classification of groups, clans and classes, interests and aspirations, régimes and organisations must take account of the factors that give rise to and destroy them, and of the mechanisms that, in a changing and, if not solidary, at any rate interdependent world, sustain this process.

The literature coming from or relating to Latin America is vast and is increasing year by year. As sociologists, demographers, anthropologists and economists, both Latin American and foreign, attempt to discover and understand this fascinating and tormented world, general impressions give way to works of analysis and evaluation. Scholarly research cautiously eschews generalisations, but the accumulation of knowledge does not of itself provide the answers sought by those anxious to determine their own future. Thus, alongside meticulous descriptions of particular social or technical aspects of reality, essays and pamphlets proliferate and provide comprehensive interpretations of events all the more categorical for their indifference to empirical detail.

It is hazardous, when one does not possess the accumulated data that make possible the understanding of situations in European and other industrial societies, to attempt an analysis of the essential structures of these complex societies, of their functioning and their evolution. There is, nevertheless, no alternative, and in undertaking the task one can but hope that one's mistakes will be of use to those who make the attempt afterwards. The data collected and the conclusions offered by the social sciences, and comparisons—where appropriate—with the historical experiences of Europe and the United States must be supplemented by direct observation, and the analysis will have to rest on provisional hypotheses derived from the comparison of heterogeneous elements, hypotheses whose confirmation, modification or abandonment can only be determined by subsequent systematic verification.

The first and indispensable step is to reject, or modify substantially, the formulas and theoretical frameworks derived from Anglo-American or European situations and employed by both foreign observers and Latin American intellectuals. Serafino Romualdi, director of the Inter-American Regional Organisation of Workers (ORIT), the regional branch of the International Confederation of Free Trade Unions, declares that 'in Latin America the class struggle is a thing of the past'; Paul Sweezy and Leo Huberman, left-wing intellectuals in this case, define the Cuban revolution as 'a dictatorship of the proletariat'. Both are equally far from the truth. These are phrases that indicate an intention or a hope, but describe and explain nothing unless it be those who utter them.

Struggles, tensions and social pressures are a permanent feature in every Latin American country. To live there or even to read the Latin American press is enough to convince one of the fact. But this does not imply any correspondence with the tactics and organisation of industrial societies, if only because the social stratification is different and classes and groups do not correspond, either in size or in function, to their theoretical equivalents in developed societies. This, while not excluding the existence of privileged and oppressed, of conflicts and problems, does mean that the features of domination and exploitation, of struggles and of developments, are markedly different in these societies.

I

Classes

1. *Decline of the Oligarchy: Persistence of the Oligarchic Spirit*

The term 'oligarchy'—frequently used to describe a type of régime common in many parts of Latin America—brings together under one label different forms of power and behaviour; a more precise definition would take account of the different historical and social contexts of its existence. By oligarchy one usually understands a system of real power whose essential dimension is economic and is based on large land-holdings. Its influence is preponderant in state affairs. The government, the civil service, the police, the army and the diplomatic service, swayed by family loyalties and clan alliances, and subject to the manipulation of *clientelae*, are no more than instruments that serve the interests of the landed proprietors.

In his study of the Peruvian oligarchy, François Bourricaud makes the following observations: 'Were one to analyse the phenomenon more deeply, one would be tempted to conclude that the most important value for an oligarch, even in its economic aspects, is power rather than efficiency.'[1] 'The observer who attempts to evaluate the functioning of the great oligarchic "empires" is struck by their low productivity and poor organisation. What counts, for an oligarch, is political influence, for among other benefits this enables him to obtain the highest degree of tariff protection.'[2]

The origin of this power, and its form, derive from the

5

encomienda system, whereby the king of Spain, sole master of the lands and inhabitants of the New World, granted land and native labour-power to individual *encomenderos* charged with the collection of taxes. Rights of administration frequently became property rights, and, fed by grants of land from the king in recognition of services rendered, the number of large agricultural estates increased. Independence cut ties with Madrid, and the landowning families, freed from their obligations, became a ruling class, experienced and solidly implanted.

Although the agrarian societies of Latin America did not remain immobile, social change, the development of manufacturing, the coming of the machine age, the extension of mining activities and external influences effected no fundamental change either in the forms of exploitation or in the nature of property. The heads of the landowning families, whether they reared cattle or grew cereals, had created individual societies in the territories they controlled. They were masters of the land and of those who lived on it. They were the only source of real authority over immense areas. They, and they alone, provided links with the town, the capital, and the state authorities. They constituted the axis of all social life. Many features of the following description still remain true at the local level.

Rio Hacha, following the example of other Colombian towns, has modelled its constitution along republican lines. The governor or president, who at the time of my stay there was an ironmonger and tortoise-shell merchant, was charged with executing the law, transmitting reports to the central government, keeping the public archives and making official acts public. Like the judges and other officials, he is elected by majority vote. The Chamber of Representatives, made up of potentates from the villages and hamlets of the province, meets in an old half-ruined church pompously named *Palacio de la Libertad*.

Like all assemblies the world over, this one, which contains twenty-four members, is divided into left, centre and right. This last fraction, made up mainly of rich landowners, is generally satisfied with the way things are going and tries to avoid all discussion that is not on the agenda. It holds a majority of the votes. The left, less disciplined and smaller in number, succeeds notwithstanding in having put to the vote all proposals of public interest, thanks to the support it derives from the young men and from the *intermittent* newspaper published by the Liberals.[3]

Despite their modified situation, and although the nature anddimensions of new problems inevitably bring them face to face with the need for change, the oligarchic groups continue to display a remarkable ability to keep their authority intact.

In March 1964 the defenders of the status quo in Chile, a governmental coalition of Conservatives, Liberals and Radicals, expected their candidate to triumph in the forthcoming presidential elections. But a key by-election in an essentially agricultural constituency where they had hoped for an easy victory was won by the candidate of the Frente de Acción Popular (FRAP), a radical Socialist-Communist grouping. The coalition political headquarters panicked. The Chilean oligarchy began a long defensive campaign. First, it withdrew from the electoral field. There would be no candidate of the right in the presidential elections. Jorge Prat, the strong man who had undertaken to renew the *caudillo* tradition by gathering round himself the underprivileged masses, was forced to withdraw through lack of support. The Radical Julio Durán put himself forward on behalf of his own party with an eye to keeping future possibilities open. Second—and despite appearances this did not contradict the first strategy—the loyal pro-government press, making good use of statements by some of the more militant Radicals, launched a vigorous campaign against FRAP, couched in emotional and polemical terms and designed not so much to discuss the merits of the rival programmes as to present the election in black-and-white terms.

With the triumph of the Christian Democrats by more than an absolute majority the danger of a 'popular front' government, in which the pro-Castro elements would have come to the fore, was removed. The tactical efforts of the traditional politicians were then aimed at electing a Chamber of Deputies which could prevent the president-elect from carrying out his programme of reforms. This hope, too, was shattered by the Christian Democrat landslide.

There remained, however, a last resort. In the senate, whose ranks were only partially renewed, the Radicals retained a stronghold. This, then, was to be the scene of a war of attrition to prevent the passing of laws that would modify the old structures.

Faced with a situation in which the solid mass of public opinion had affirmed its desire for change (the Christian Democrat and FRAP vote combined amounted to three-quarters of the electorate), the oligarchy manoeuvred with remarkable tenacity. Its efforts were directed not against the measures relating to the Chileanisation of copper (increased production, development of ore processing on national soil, expansion of trade with all possible customers) but against the land reform. Legalistic quibbling, alarmist campaigns, the mobilisation of all available pens and voices—from eminent economists to literary critics—all these means were brought into play simultaneously or one after another. Within the ranks of the Christian Democrats themselves a more subtle campaign was launched, aimed at neutralising the will to change by emphasising now one aspect and now another of the whole question and by this accumulation of misrepresentations creating confusion and exploiting the latent conflicts of interest that had been submerged by the appeal of the comprehensive programme of reforms.

A closing of the Christian Democrat ranks and a reaffirmation of loyalty to the programme were necessary before a new minister (Jaime Castillo Velasco, one of the intellectual leaders of the movement), could be appointed, charged with the public warding off of a double attack: that of the Socialists and Communists on the one hand, aimed at destroying the unity of the Christian Democrat coalition, and that of the landed interests on the other, which used all possible means and excuses to multiply delays.

Two further examples will illustrate the extent and limits of oligarchic power today. In Ecuador, and above all in its mountain region, agricultural land is in the hands of a few hundred families. Most of the land under cultivation is in holdings of over 500 hectares (1,270 acres). Apparently legitimate legal relationships conceal the existence of serfdom. Farm labourers and share-croppers—paid either in cash or in kind, or by being allowed to cultivate a small plot of land, or again under some combination of these methods—the local terms are *huasipungueros*, *zanaperos*, *aparceros* and *medieros*—are tied to the estate by the power of the landowner and by accumulated debts. The existence of thousands of small land-holdings, meagre for the most part, does not constitute a contradiction, in economic terms, with the predominance of the *latifundio* system. They are frequently directly dependent on the power of the owner of the large estate, those who live on them making up a labour force that is readily available for economic or political ends and which in addition costs nothing. The situation is the same as that of Mexico after the Spanish conquest, as described by the American anthropologist Eric Wolf in speaking of the relations between Indian communities and the Spanish administration of confiscated land: 'Assured of seasonal laborers who would do their bidding at the critical periods in the process of production, the *haciendas* welcomed the presence of Indian communities on their fringes. For such a community constituted a convenient reservoir of laborers where men maintained their labor power until needed, at no additional cost to the entrepreneur.'[4]

Wolf's analysis of the economic rôle of the *hacienda* and of the *hacendado*'s mentality in eighteenth-century Mexico could also be applied to present-day situations and forms of behaviour:

The *hacienda* played safe by always producing below capacity. It never staked all or even most of its land on the vagaries of the market. In times of uncertainty, it could always fall back on its own resources and feed itself. It possessed its own defences, which it never jeopardized. Inefficient in its use of land, it was yet greedy for it. It needed and wanted more land, not to raise more crops, but to take land from the Indians in order to force them to leave their holdings and to become dependent on the *hacienda* for land and work.[5]

The Brazilian *fazenda* provides another good illustration. Labour was scarce, and this induced the landowner to allow landless peasants to cultivate a small plot for their subsistence on his estate; in exchange, he had a readily available labour force at his disposal when it was required. The *fazendeiro* protected his peasants against neighbouring landowners and the federal government; conversely this *clientela* was an army which the landowner could employ—in fact or as a threat—against his rivals and in his dealings with the state.

Political change had no fundamental effect on the working of this closed society. The landowner became an important member of the electorate: the number of votes he controlled gave him influence in the towns and in the state or federal capital. He bargained with it and obtained subsidies or credit with which to increase his local power.

Neither the assertion of their rights by social groups nor local revolts—which invariably clustered round a central figure, a new patron, whose charisma soon turned him into a landowner himself—produced any important change. Progressive absenteeism created new relationships between the overseer (now the sole representative of the landowner on the estate) and the peasants, who were now isolated and defenceless. Particularly after 1930, the landowners moved to the towns where commercial and other activities offered them greater benefits than did their estates. As the population of the towns increased, prices of agricultural goods rose, but middlemen siphoned off the increase and prices paid to the peasant producer remained static. The relatively sparse population increased disproportionately with agricultural incomes, and seasonal migration of agricultural labour became necessary.

Old ties were broken and the closed society of the *fazenda* became more open. New forms of organisation, solidarity and security replaced the old patron-client relationship, but the peasant leagues (*ligas camponesas*) that have recently emerged in north-east Brazil do not represent the growth of a revolutionary 'peasant class consciousness'. Set free from their old ties, the landless masses became available for manipulation by new protectors operating in the political sphere. Francisco Julião, the lawyer who was at the head of the movement, and his agents (students from the cities) attempted to replace the *fazendeiro* and become intermediaries between the local or regional peasant population and the state or federal authorities. By using the potential threat offered by the peasants as political capital, they obtained from the authorities credit and emergency measures. The *clientela* that had previously depended on the landowner now became a political *clientela* in the hands of the government. The new leaders are manipulators, not instruments, and the oligarchic tradition survives in the new situation.[6]

The inheritor of this tradition has a solid base for his local power in the long tradition of direct government. His relatives and his friends are strategically placed in the administration. He owns considerable capital. The sources of information are largely in his hands. In his own way he has come to terms with the need to industrialise and face competition in international trade. And yet his rule is no longer absolute. More and more he is faced with obstacles he can neither eliminate nor bypass. The classical instruments of oligarchic power—the army and the university among others—have evolved in their own way and are now autonomous foci of power. His faithful, dependent and grateful *clientelae* became blocs of votes and later the 'ultimate weapon' in political bargaining: maintenance of the past no longer holds any meaning for them. Decisions are taken not in the *haciendas* or the *fundos*, but in the towns, and towns cannot be manoeuvred as could a dependent population of clients.

Even in those countries where it still enjoys solid prerogatives, the oligarchy is no longer in sole command. Too many now aspire to power. The oligarchs can still protect themselves, manoeuvre, and sometimes mediate. Their last trump is the lack of any rival class sufficiently powerful, united or equipped with a modern political machine.

No longer dominant, the oligarchy sees its spirit and manners copied by its social and political opponents. Disdain for manual work, contempt for the Indian, the pride and conviction of belonging to an élite are no longer exclusive to the oligarchy. They are part of a heritage that is claimed or aspired to—with varying degrees of hypocrisy—by most of the groups who aim at political power, even when they make a great show of their revolutionary principles, their admiration for the ancient Indian civilisation, or their devotion to fulfilling the historic mission of the proletarian masses. In Mexico City or in Lima one would be hard put to find a bank clerk or a student, no matter how radical his politics, who would degrade himself by carrying a parcel or do without a large number of servants—kept, of course, at an Indian standard of living. Whoever succeeds in escaping from the working class or the peasantry immediately dreams of entering the world of many-faceted power, the world of the oligarchic spirit.

Those who today aspire to power project a type of society that seems to have nothing in common with the seigneurial domain where the master, at the centre of his realm, was in complete control. The slogans are increased productivity, rationalisation, the development of natural resources. But the pyramidal form of the power structure of the new groupings, and the attitudes of those at the top, are strangely akin to those of the despised and envied oligarchy.

The oligarchic influence has permeated even the cultural sphere. Liberalism is closer to paternalism than to egalitarianism. The scholar, the teacher and the writer defend their position of pre-eminence against all those who presume to occupy it, and above all against the younger generation, who are accepted as pupils and disciples but seldom as successors or potential peers.

The methods of politics are imbued with the oligarchic spirit. Many parties which profess democratic doctrines are dominated by families or solidary groups which overshadow assemblies and congresses—less centres of tactical decisions than display places for those who hold the real power.

All this suggests that a suitably oriented study might find that most economic, social and political phenomena in Latin America reveal the same mechanisms of dependence, perpetuating, from colonial times to the present day, the Hispanic tradition.

2. *A Marginal and Dependent Bourgeoisie*

The bourgeoisie of the capitalist enterprises is not the dominant class; it has no determining say in the conduct of state affairs; it is, for the most part, foreign or of foreign descent. In other words, the industrial revolution did not take place in most Latin American countries. Industrial development is frequently the result of foreign initiatives, foreign technology, and foreign capital.

In Chile, the pioneering spirit appeared after independence and an important industrial and mining sector was created. But soon a kind of languor took hold of the owners, who became more interested in enjoying the fruits of their commercial and handicraft activities than in investing the profits and developing a manufacturing industry. The most striking example of this decadence is provided by the handing over to foreign mining companies of the rich nitrate areas that had been seized from Peru.

The heart of the question is this: Chilean entrepreneurs and workers discover and make a decisive contribution to the development of the wealth of the plain. The foreign states whose territory this is attempt to reduce or eliminate Chilean participation. Our country, conscious of its deeply-rooted rights and of the potential importance of nitrate for a declining export economy, makes the supreme sacrifice of going to war. It is victorious, and immediately takes measures that soon snatch the fruits of this conquest from national control.[7]

That the government of the time should have been able not only to accept but to suggest such a policy is sufficient indication that there did not exist—or no longer existed—in Chile an audacious and dynamic industrial bourgeoisie. The small manufacturing plants themselves—textile and others—did not develop so that they could face up to international competition. In 1910, 5,780 firms employed almost 75,000 workers; by 1923 concentration had reduced the number of firms to about 3,200, whereas the labour-force employed had only risen to 82,000.

For a long time, imports of luxury goods were to exceed those of machines and equipment. The degree to which the landowning class, the proprietors of large agricultural estates or of the mines, are opposed to change is reflected in the policies of the governments which they make or control.

The vacuum they create is only partly filled by foreign companies, and these are only interested in primary produce or in enterprises that yield quick profits. A balanced economic development of the countries in which they operate is no concern of theirs. The spirit of capitalism is introduced, maintained and illustrated by immigrants who are enterprising by necessity, who create or develop commercial and industrial enterprises, but who have no means of influencing power politics.

When change becomes a necessity as a country's backwardness relative to the rest of the world becomes apparent, there is no bourgeoisie sufficiently experienced and daring to carry it out of its own accord and according to its own methods. There is then room for a new social stratum to make itself evident. Should the need arise, this class could mobilise the accumulated nationalistic bitterness of a population which sees in economic development nothing more than a source of profit for the Yankee, the Jew, the Italian or the Turco.* The Chilean case is the most striking example of a social class—the bourgeoisie—refusing, as it were, to perform a social rôle when the opportunity and the material means of doing so were available. But it is not the only example.

A study of Argentine industrial associations, carried out by the sociologist José Luis de Imaz, provides evidence of the same nature. Given the fact that the countries of the Plate basin received large numbers of immigrants, whereas Chile's geographical isolation led to a rapid stabilisation of the population's racial composition, it comes as no surprise to find that the Argentine Industrial Union was founded in 1887 by a small number of Argentine *criollos* and an overwhelming majority of foreigners. Nor is it remarkable that, in 1894, 85 per cent of the 23,000 firms should have been owned by Italians, French and Germans. But when one finds that in 1961 the majority of the business élite—managers of Argentine subsidiaries of foreign corporations, the most important leaders of industry and those with the highest prestige—was not Argentine, one begins to realise the significance of the fact that the country's industrial development was produced by a will that had no roots in the country itself. 'Thus', concludes the study, 'it becomes clear that the shock troops, the vanguard of Argentine enterprise, are largely made up of non-Argentines.'[8]

Even in countries where immigration has never taken place on a large scale, the proportion of foreign businessmen is high. This, for example, is the case in Colombia, where a survey carried out in 1962 revealed that 41 per cent of Bogotá entrepreneurs were foreigners.[9]

．　　　．　　　．

* Turco is a term applied indiscriminately to immigrants from the Middle East, most of whom are in fact Syrians or Lebanese.

Where, as in Brazil or Peru, a young and vigorous managerial sector is in evidence, one cannot speak of a *class*, of a social sector with its own characteristics, expressing and defending a common interest, conscious of its own particular rôle and destiny. As economic activity takes on an industrial character, and to the degree that private initiative lies behind or plays a prominent part in it, two types of entrepreneur appear. The first is attached to the traditionally privileged classes—to the oligarchy, in other words—by its origins, by kinship ties, and by its attitudes.

Prefacing a study carried out for the National Planning Association (United States), Theodore Geiger describes this sector as follows:

> This older type of enterprise has largely developed over the past 50 years or more in the older industrial and commercial fields—*e.g.*, textiles and clothing, processed foods and beverages, other light consumer goods, money-lending, and foreign trade. The technology of these industries was comparatively simple and changed relatively slowly, particularly in the decades when they were first established in Latin America. The markets which these industries served were small and slow-growing, and the factors which entrepreneurs had to take into account were relatively simple.[10]

There was thus no need either for technical or professional training or for long-term forecasting. This type of enterprise was no more than a dependent extension of the interests of the oligarchic families.

> The essential goal of the enterprise was to provide the income with which to maintain and improve the status, the income and the standard of living of the family or the small group of associated proprietors of the business. Large immediate profits were generally preferred to the reinvestment of profits in the

long-term improvement and expansion of the firm. Managerial positions and responsibilities were usually reserved for
members of the family.[11]

The youngest members of the family prepared themselves for
succession in the firm without going through the university or
the professional schools.

The other type of entrepreneur is more recent: he is interested
in modern techniques of producing chemicals, synthetic materials, machinery, electric equipment. The conditions of production
and the market themselves impel him to operate and plan in
terms of new techniques. He tends to be equipped with a solid
professional training, to think in terms of development, to be at
the head of a group of shareholders whose funds come from many
sources, preferably from a group of relatives or friends.

This phenomenon is easily seen in Peru, where the ever-present
families 'make money' in cement, building and export-import
firms as well as in real estate or agriculture, while young entrepreneurs attempt to create specialised industries whose operation
becomes the focus of their activity and their hopes. From a
survey made between 1959 and 1963 on the activities of entrepreneurs in fourteen Latin American countries, Albert Lauterbach was able to conclude:

1. The widespread lack of specialization in a definite industry
or field of business: The same person, family group, or office frequently administers a variety of enterprises which may range
from textile plants and sugar plantations to mines and banks.

2. The interconnection of business and management with
family relationships and politics: Managers are frequently
selected on the basis of family links, rather than specialized
training. They constantly use political influence in order to get
things done or to secure special favors for their companies. A
business manager may also put in a short period of service as
public administrator or cabinet minister without necessarily

discontinuing his interests in private business. Money made through the political medium may go into new or old enterprises and the *político* may transform himself into an entrepreneur.[12]

It is clear that the social and political ideas of these two groups of entrepreneurs are widely divergent and frequently opposed to one another. The liberal laissez-faire mentality of the former corresponds to a desire to use a 'policeman state' to guarantee social stability and a government of friends as far as business is concerned. The technological sensitivity of the latter leads them to want a state interested in creating the preconditions of national or even regional development, of which the entrepreneur would be the mainspring.

A similar situation can be found in several parts of Brazil, where the interests and horizons of the 'traditional' entrepreneurs —those connected to the landowners, and generally favouring the status quo or a 'natural evolution' of things—have little in common with those of the new industrialists, the product largely of recent immigration, who see the tradition of the old local families as an obstacle to the development of the country and the building up of a large internal market.

When one allows for the low level of industrialisation and for the lack of enthusiasm with which the privileged classes view their voluntary participation in the economic 'take-off', and when one observes how, even within the managerial stratum, origin (national or foreign), training (family or technical), class ties (oligarchy or independent) and political ideas (a state to guarantee order or a state to foster development) lead to divergent configurations and prospects, one recognises the absurdity of speaking of a 'capitalist class'. It is even more difficult to sift out an orientation common to the 'entrepreneurial bourgeoisie' which might be capable of imposing itself on the state.

To be sure, when news arrives from the villages that peasants are demonstrating or have taken over more land, the same fear haunts the residential districts of Lima. The cleavage thus divides landed proprietors with a direct stake in the status quo from capitalists who would like to see the integration of the Indian population into national life. Here, as in Brazil, Chile or Venezuela, land reform is the key issue.

Conceptions of the state and its rôle vary considerably among the different sections—who constitute minorities, one must remember—of the capitalist bourgeoisie, but the oldest governing élite, which for generations has provided the rulers and made or destroyed governments, still enjoys a considerable tactical advantage. To return to the Chilean example, the events of the last few decades provide many illustrations of the skill and resilience of the old oligarchy, which has been able to erect barriers against any reform movement, but which displays equal skill, when the electoral tide turns against it, in adapting itself to the new situation without sacrificing any of its prerogatives or changing its ways.

So much is this so that one finds enterprising elements of the bourgeoisie forced in their turn to play the frequently dangerous political game of allying themselves with non-oligarchic or even anti-oligarchic groups thrown up by events or movements that reflect conflicts deeper and more complex than those of economic interests alone. Thus, in Argentina, the Confederación General Económica, which is made up largely of provincial entrepreneurs, joined the Peronist movement and was duly rewarded, while the old Unión Industrial, politically liberal, and conservative as far as social questions were concerned, joined the opposition.

One characteristic is shared by both sections—a concern with the power of the state—but whereas the oligarchic groups, which include the entrepreneurs associated with them, aim to reduce the rôle of the state to that of guardian of the established order, the younger capitalists are anxious to collaborate and participate in a general development policy which only the state is able to formulate and implement.

One must beware, therefore, of confusing interest groups which, while bearing the same name and coming under the same ideological rubric, perform or could perform opposing rôles in any given social or political situation. And the nature of the state in Latin America makes caution all the more necessary. Far from always being simply an instrument, the state is a powerful— sometimes the most powerful—economic agent in society.

Without taking account of the 'imported' character of Latin American industry, one cannot understand the attitudes and behaviour of private and public entrepreneurs. Right from the beginning, and even when local or national conditions were favourable in one way or another, development has been based on European or North American models.

International trade and technical standards are determined by an organised market over which Latin American producers or clients have only marginal influence. For a long time, the structure of the subcontinent's economies was extremely elementary: internal circuits that ensured the distribution of food and provided for the limited needs of a small population, and an export sector producing primary products.

As the Brazilian sociologist Fernando Henrique Cardoso remarks:

> The connection between the market (which was *foreign* and which had existed . . . from the very earliest days of Latin American history) and the local interests was mediated through the State, which was itself curtailed either by the non-productive local oligarchy or by the landowning producers, to the exclusion of the other classes and social groups.[13]

The first modifications were to be introduced from abroad: systematic cultivation introduced by North American companies in Central America; modern exploitation of mineral resources in Chile, Peru and Bolivia, and of oil in Venezuela and Mexico. It was the import restrictions on manufactured goods, as a consequence of the two World Wars, that gave birth to national industry or allowed it to develop. With the return of peace, local production was to retreat in the face of the return of the great international corporations who could offer superior goods produced by advanced techniques developed in vast and organised markets.

The initiation of a general process of industrialisation growing from a desire for independence, can under these conditions no longer be undertaken by imaginative and successful small capitalists, as it was in the nineteenth century. To quote Cardoso once again, 'When the entrepreneur groups came to the fore there was already an active state organization and an established market, and the other social forces—the urban masses and middle-class groups, the oligarchies and exporters—were competing for control of the state machinery, and thus for the possibility of influencing decisions relating to investment and consumption.'[14]

3. *Middle Classes* ad infinitum

The middle classes are frequently mentioned in the literature devoted to Latin America. Many observers believe that they are the moving force behind political progress. It is hard to locate them. One lacks definitions. The statistics, which should be able to record the importance and size of the different categories, shrink and swell according to the criteria used. For the census-takers, they represent the residue left after the working class, the agricultural labourers and the privileged classes have been accounted for. Thus one finds lumped together in this category—though sometimes distinguished by the prefixes 'upper' or 'lower' —small businessmen, tradesmen, members of the liberal professions, civil servants, old age pensioners, *rentiers*, independent peasants, and artisans.

This catch-all term is a little too comprehensive to be of much use in understanding the rôle of the middle classes in relatively unstructured societies. One should note, too, the propensity of all wage-earners who have a fixed occupation and a little education to call themselves 'middle class'. The typesetter from Buenos Aires and the Santiago taxi-driver think they belong to the middle class. So, naturally, do the bank managers and businessmen.

It is not easy to uncover their real functions in the political and economic field, or their aspirations—and objective possibilities— in the process of social change. Some countries—Uruguay, for example—seem, if one keeps to the classical definitions, to be inhabited entirely by members of the middle class. Elsewhere, they tend to merge with ethnically homogeneous groups: the *mestizo* population in Bolivia, for example.

The figures that have been assembled—which differ considerably according to source—help avoid extravagances, but, given the present state of knowledge, it is better to limit oneself to prudent generalities. Firstly, one can suggest that the towns contain the largest proportion of the middle class. Secondly, that its proliferation does not necessarily correspond to economic development or industrialisation. Thirdly, that the middle class provides the troops and militants of the political parties, who are the direct rivals of the old formations created and manipulated by the oligarchy.

These three remarks lead one to believe that the middle class constitutes an important mass of 'availables' who cannot be fully absorbed by the old structures and who provide every reformist or revolutionary movement with men and cadres.

The continued expansion of this tertiary sector, when the economy is not growing at the same rate and cannot therefore absorb it, leads the parties and the state to manipulate *clientelae*, to create jobs and parasitic functions, thus limiting, while not eliminating, the bitterness and frustrations of the younger generation. At the same time, their upkeep is costly to the public purse, thus, paradoxically, making fundamental reform more difficult.

So long as the old economic mechanisms still function, a kind of cohabitation is maintained between the oligarchy and the government services that dispense sinecures or distribute public funds in one form or another. But when a time of crisis arrives and the state can no longer afford to maintain these clients, the old system begins to show its age, and the need for reform becomes apparent. The parties representing the middle class are equally unprepared, economically and socially, to undertake fundamental changes. Frequently their decomposition and collapse accompany the revelation of the oligarchy's incapacity, for they denounce the system that keeps them alive. It is then that new formations or improvised movements arise.

There is considerable variation from country to country in the situation of the middle class. The Venezuelan case is radically different from the Uruguayan, as is the Mexican from the Chilean. Nevertheless, the decisive rôle of the middle class is common to all of them. It is the group that provides the pressure for change and demands for satisfaction. But it would be foolish to imagine that these pressures are in the direction of greater rationality, improved techniques, more efficient organisation, and a search for economic progress. The victory of the middle class, even when achieved by revolutionary means and with the support of the masses, is sometimes costly, for it implies a further extension of bureaucratic functions.

The Bolivian tin mines provide a sadly eloquent illustration. Under the rule of the *rosca*—the mining oligarchy—the ratio between the miners and the mainly administrative surface personnel was balanced. According to figures provided by the Corporación Minera de Bolivia (COMIBOL), this balance was destroyed a few years after the revolution: there were twice as many surface personnel as miners.*

In Venezuela, on the other hand, the revenues derived from

* In his *Informe de Labores*, La Paz 1960, Sinforoso Cabrera Romero, the worker-manager of COMIBOL, gives the following figures: 1952, 7,422 miners, 8,999 surface personnel; 1956, 5,587 and 12,711 respectively; and, in 1959, 5,841 and 11,080.

oil, which made possible the modernisation and industrialisation of the country, increased the demand for managerial cadres and personnel, thus paving the way for the victory of the middle-class parties, Acción Democrática and Copei.

In Uruguay, the stagnation of the international market for meat, the conservatism of cattle-breeders and economic decadence have not so far produced any disturbance among the middle class, the members of which are essentially dependants of the state.

Far from all theorising, and as a result of a series of painful and often bloody experiences that cannot be fitted systematically into any doctrinal framework, Mexico affords the clearest example of the rise to power of the middle class and its take-over of the state, with all the contradictions that it entailed.

The Chilean case likewise has its own characteristics. The collapse of the political formations used by the oligarchy may be a prelude to the demise of the economically privileged groups, and the decline of the Radical party—mouthpiece and creator of civil servants—may imply a qualitative change in the state personnel.

Common to them all is one fact: it was not the development of industrial capitalism which broke or which threatened the old structures, it was not a rising of the working or peasant masses; it is a non-productive class of qualified and unqualified intellectuals that has taken or is seeking the succession.

The factory that produces the middle class is clearly the university. Long devoted to giving the oligarchy a general education, to providing the rich families with lawyers and doctors and the schools with teachers, the university has over the past thirty or forty years taken on a new importance. Its development only occasionally follows the course of social change; it frequently seems to follow a rhythm of its own.

The great reformist movement which defined its charter in the Declaration of Córdoba (Argentina) in 1918, stated clearly the problem of the relationship between the university, students and society. But the future of this movement was to be determined less by its original communal spirit than by the fragmentary and compartmented nature of society and by the growth of the university as an autonomous organism.

Here we have another example of the incoherent and un-balanced growth of the public services. Education and the access to knowledge and culture are presented as a right which every citizen should enjoy. But the citizen who enjoys this right believes that his degree, or his studies, give him prerogatives and new rights. Furthermore, what is taught bears no relation to the precise needs appearing in society.

From this point of view, the university in its turn becomes a state institution on the same level as any other, *viz.*, a means of resisting social pressures, or at any rate of containing them. Its future is conceived independently of any connection with society as a whole but is conditioned by a series of struggles and conflicts with other badly-articulated parts of the state and society.

It would hardly be a caricature of the image presented by many Latin American universities to portray them as a badly paid teaching body, whose members consider a chair as a title supplementary to outside professional activities; students who see their studies as a means of joining the privileged classes and who are shaped by various pressures into a political force; graduates whose only future, if they do not already belong to one or another of the privileged classes, is emigration.

Research, an essential function of a university, has developed slowly and with great difficulty; that it has got under way at all is due mainly to the grants and research programmes of North American institutions.

In the expanding metropolitan capitals—in Caracas and Mexico City especially—the university centres display build-ings, parks and services whose extravagance and modernity become symbolic. The new political class, having achieved power, prepares the generations that will perpetuate it.

. . . .

Clearly, the middle class does not represent a social force with uniform aspirations and interests. Another of its elements, the state bureaucrats, frequently owe their positions to a favour granted in exchange for electoral services. They do not consider that the citizen who presents himself at the counter or in the office has the right to good service. The civil servant depends, not on the public who supports him, but on the political clan which has given him the post. The 'client' forced to turn to the administration can demand nothing. If he wants to avoid long waits, he will be well advised to go through his party, or his club—unless, that is, he can establish a personal relationship with the 'public servant' on the basis of friendship or a bribe. That he be a tradesman, an artisan, a lawyer or a professor—in other words, of the same 'class' as the representative of the administration—does not affect the situation.

To take another case, there is more solidarity between a banker and a bank clerk than between the clerk and a depositor, or a man in the street who needs some banking service. Most action taken by associations of bank employees aims at sharing in the profits made by the employers, not in proposing a reform of the banking system, even when this is indisputably based on exploitation.

Sections of the middle class can thus, in certain situations, ally themselves with clearly oligarchic groups, while others support movements that aim at change. But it would be hard to find a party which—leaving aside the promises of favours which power would permit them to grant—could present a programme *of the middle class* which would give it a mission and outline for it a future tied to the development of the country.

4. *Land without Peasants*

In Bolivia, more than half the population is employed in agriculture. In Mexico, the percentage is 57 per cent; in Brazil, 60 per cent; in Venezuela, 41 per cent; in Peru, 62 per cent; in Chile, nearly 30 per cent; and in Argentina, over 25 per cent.

The figures refer to 1950, but they are to a large extent still valid. They reveal the nature of the Latin American subcontinent, but they also disguise a complex reality that admits of few generalisations.

Generally speaking, one can say that from the point of view of production, agriculture and cattle-rearing were oriented towards exports, and internal markets were neglected. This trend is closely linked to the forms of landholding. The large estates belonging to the traditional families were cultivated with a foreign, mainly European, market in mind. A closed circuit satisfied the subsistence requirements of the workers who lived on the estate, whether they were directly linked to the master's 'society' or were allowed to cultivate a plot for their own needs. At the other extreme—there were virtually no medium-sized holdings—the tiny *minifundios* produced barely enough for their owners' subsistence.

The overpopulation of the urban centres, the increase in domestic consumption, greater competition from new centres of production elsewhere in the world, the improved quality required by international markets and the development of the trade in industrially processed agricultural goods had little effect on agriculture and cattle-raising. They remained traditional and made no attempt to adapt to the changing situation. Absolute stagnation in a changing context implied a relative decline. Falling sales in international markets reduced the amounts of foreign exchange available for importing industrial products and materials, and accentuated under-development. The volume of exports was declining, for the domestic market consumed an increasing proportion of a static production. Monoculture led to imports of food, which further reduced the possibilities of using exchange derived from exports to speed up industrialisation. Paradoxes became frequent: the price of food in the cities became prohibitive, while manufactured goods produced in the cities could not be sold in the rural areas because incomes were so low.

Agriculture has developed slowly, if we except those producers who were near enough to the cities to market their products easily and reinvest the profits in their farms, the few large land-owners who have tried to modernise and adapt to the conditions of international markets and the few immigrant families or colonies which have transplanted, to regions whose soil had been previously studied, techniques and machinery tested in Europe or North Africa. Far from becoming more flexible and adapting to the changed situation, forms of land tenure have tended to coalesce at the two equally disastrous extremes of the *latifundio* and the *minifundio*.

Figures published in 1957 by the International Labour Organisation reveal that in Argentina the large estates covered 46·2 per cent, while individual plots—over 36 per cent of the number of landholdings—covered less than 1 per cent of the total area under cultivation. And yet this is the country in which a peasant middle class is coming into being in the peripheral provinces, mainly in Chubut, La Pampa and Rio Negro.

In Chile, the 1955 census figures show that the large estates—2 per cent of the holdings—covered 40 per cent of the cultivable area, while individual plots of under 5 hectares (12½ acres), which represented over a quarter of the number of holdings, covered 1·7 per cent. Small and medium landholdings, the former averaging 11 hectares (27 acres), the latter between 50 (125 acres) and 1,000 (2,500 acres) were reasonably developed. In Venezuela, in 1956, properties of more than 1250 acres covered over half of the cultivated land, whereas those of less than 25 acres made up 83 per cent of the holdings.

These statistics cannot give any idea of what is implied for social relations and ways of life. One must consider also the fertility of the soil, the distance from markets, the level of education of those who work the land, and their standard of living and degree of dependence. Thus, no matter how laudable one's intentions, one must beware of reformist or revolutionary slogans that are made up in the cities and meant to apply to the rural areas. In the Uruguayan elections of 1962, an extreme left-wing group included in its programme the high-sounding but meaningless formula: 'The land for those who work it.' For even if there are in fact large estates in Uruguay, these are given over to cattle rearing and not to agriculture. The scattered *gaucho* population would not be anxious to cultivate the plains where the cattle roam.

Distant observers tend to have an image of the Latin American peasantry that rarely corresponds to reality. Labour furnished in cutting sugar-cane, or in picking coffee and fruit, as a temporary wage-earner or as a worker attached to the landowner's household, on whose domain a hut and a plot of land have been allotted to him in exchange for labour of different kinds— conditions such as these do not produce a peasant, a producer closely tied to the land who knows the possibilities open to him and engages in exchange with other sectors of society. The question of land reform—a reform that is necessary and unavoidable—is also the question of the creation of a peasantry.

The paralysis of systems of land tenure and methods of agricultural production at a time when the other sectors of society are changing produces a series of phenomena which accentuate social and economic imbalances and create new problems. One of the main consequences of the stagnation of rural society is migration towards the urban centres. The owner of a small plot that is not sufficient for the minimum needs of his family, and the would-be owner who knows that so long as he continues to work on another's land he has no chance of obtaining even the smallest plot, go to the towns in search of temporary employment, aiming to accumulate a small reserve to complement what they earn in the country. These two types of temporary or seasonal migrants want nothing more than to return under improved conditions. On the other hand, agricultural labourers or the sons of large families go to the cities intending to remain. They go to swell the population of unemployed or semi-employed in the 'zones' that surround the built-up parts of the city. The fluidity of the population which these movements create contrasts with the rigidity of the traditional structures.

As the sociologists would put it, the difficulty or impossibility of vertical mobility in the community of origin produces horizontal mobility. The social and political consequences are considerable: in most cases the urban centres cannot absorb the incoming labour-force. Problems of employment, housing, sanitation and planning multiply. The budgets of the city authorities, the development of industry, and town planning programmes cannot cope with the swelling population. A large category of 'availables', comparable to that which exists in the middle class, is rapidly created among the lower strata.

This stirring of populations hitherto embedded in traditional ways of life and thought is of particular importance in the Andean countries with a large Indian population, in Ecuador, Peru and Bolivia. The Indian communities, whose lands have been continually and until very recently whittled away, amputated and confiscated, are to be found mainly in the more distant and arid regions. Even if they still represent the tradition of the pre-Columbian *ayllu* collectives and recover some of their vigour when it comes to defending their interests they cannot be considered as a basis for large-scale organisation. Nor can they be held to represent the characteristic form of Indian society. They are nothing but pockets of resistance, the residual debris of an ancient society.

In Ecuador, the Indians constitute 40 per cent of the population and are located mainly in the mountain areas. In Peru, they represent the same proportion—the proportion rising with increased altitude; whereas, in Bolivia, they make up 55 per cent of the total population.

Their geographical isolation from the urban centres, their closed-circuit economy, their position of dependence and the marginal nature of their civilisation as embodied in their language and their customs, have given them the appearance of a distinctive population, present but non-participant. The Bolivian

Revolution of 1952, the rise of *mestizos* in political life, and changes in social mechanisms in Peru have led to 'the great stirring', to a greater mobility of the Indian populations. The suburbs of the cities and new industrial centres now have a largely Indian population.

The phase of integration has begun and it involves countless dramas, tensions and struggles. But one must be on one's guard against romanticising the situation and realise that this integration means first of all the disintegration of what remains of Indian society.

5. *A Non-conquering Working Class*

Can one speak of a 'working class' in the context of countries that are wholly or partly non-industrial? In Ecuador or Paraguay, the workers are few in number, and are found only in sectors such as printing, food-processing, transport, the docks and construction. Apart from a few craftsmen—typesetters, mechanics or carpenters—most are *peones*, unskilled labourers, employed in the few workshops and factories. Employment in these essentially agricultural regions is a blessing in itself.

In those countries which after the middle of the nineteenth century developed industries to supply the internal market or to process for export—Argentina, Uruguay, Chile and Brazil—associations came into being, and with them particular forms of behaviour and organisation. A small but active and participant working class was formed, largely through the influence of immigrants who brought with them outlooks, forms of association, tactics and hopes for a new society. This workers' movement was made up in essence of nuclei of qualified workers who had some professional capital: naval refitters in Buenos Aires, hat-makers, tailors, specialists in livestock slaughtering and skinning in the large meat processing establishments of the River Plate, tile and mosaic craftsmen, painters, carpenters, stonemasons, printers, sailors and railwaymen. This working class is in many aspects similar to the working class at the turn of the century in

Europe. In Chile, the same beginnings of industry led to a parallel development. The first trade unions were those of the printers, the shoe-makers, and bricklayers. The country's geographical position led to a reinforcing of American ideological influences by European ones transmitted through Argentina. The large cities of Brazil—Rio, São Paulo, Santos—experienced essentially the same developments.

In addition to the urban workers, who belonged to a tradition of trade unions, working-class islands came into being in the mining areas, copper and phosphate in Chile, tin in Bolivia, lead in Peru. These workers, most of whom were of peasant origin but who also absorbed a number of 'swallows' from the towns, have had their own peculiar experiences and have produced organisations which, despite the changes that have taken place in other sectors of society, still preserve their own distinctive characteristics.

In the urban centres, this working class was to be influenced by several factors. Firstly, the opportunities of mobility offered by a new society were to deprive it of some of its most useful members, who set up a workshop and small industry or went into commerce or politics. Secondly, the growth of industry increased the number of unqualified and assembly-line workers. Thirdly, state enterprises were later to become employment banks for electoral clients. Lastly, and most importantly, large-scale migration and the influx of large numbers of workless ex-peasants were to reduce and in part neutralise the importance of this organised craft-based working class.

From then on—and this is true mainly of Argentina and Brazil—the élite character and revolutionary dynamism of the working-class organisations were to fade and disappear. The mass of the *lumpenproletariat* became important, and their potential energy came to be channelled and used in the power struggle.

A pre-industrial or barely industrial society characterised by an oligarchy and by raw material production for export produces one type of working class. Social changes produced by the increase of population, the coming into play of independent sources of power, the side-effects of economic crises and the effects of two World Wars, imply a new working class with its own distinctive attitudes and characteristics.

In the Argentine wage-earning stratum, one can easily find a spectrum reflecting different periods and testifying to the survival of yesterday's working class embedded in today's. Far from disappearing, the earlier industries still represent an easily recognisable sector—for example, in Buenos Aires, printers, railwaymen, commercial employees and certain building trades such as the famous plumbers, zinc roofers and sanitary workers; shoe-makers and plasterers in Chile; and printing trade workers of São Paulo.

When, however, one adds together these diverse elements and places them in a framework that is still largely agrarian, one finds not one homogeneous working class, but two distinct working classes corresponding to two distinct periods of time. In the continually growing cities the masses of would-be workers expect from the powerful—be it a *caudillo* or a populist party, a dictatorship or a parliamentary régime—not rights and duties, but guarantees and security.

Social legislation passed by parliaments or decreed by authoritarian régimes frequently reflects the ambiguity of government policies as regards the working classes, an ambiguity that can be explained by the two stages of the working-class movement: conquering in its first phase, dependent in the second. Using *justicialista*, labourist or socialist terminology, it bears witness to a clear desire to prevent the development of an autonomous workers' movement and to integrate the energies of the working class within the state machine, not so much in order to allow it to participate in economic life as to have it reinforce a fragile and unsupported power.

In Chile, for example, most social legislation favoured administrative, commercial and office employees, the preferred

33

electoral clients of the competing Conservative and Radical parties. The unions, on the other hand, were hemmed in by texts that placed them under state control and left them prey to the management. Their only safeguard was a degree of political protection. Trade union activity can only take place through unofficial organisations whose lack of legal status does not affect their solidity. Those, agricultural workers in particular, who were held to represent a potential threat to the social structure were refused the right to strike. Taken as a whole, this legislation both contributed to the maintenance of the status quo and allowed the political parties to treat the unions as colonies. As the centres of decision-making came to be increasingly concentrated in public administration and in parliaments, one finds a continual absorption of union militants by multiple political and state organisations, the militant being transformed into an official or unofficial public servant.

In Brazil and Argentina, *getulismo* and *peronismo*, two hybrid political formulas which nevertheless represent an attempt to fuse previously separate social forces into a single national policy, strove to mobilise, absorb and use the new urban masses. Making good use of favourable economic circumstances, Getúlio Vargas and Juan Perón obtained the support of the proletarian masses by means of a series of measures guaranteeing wages, setting up pension schemes, and organising social security. Based on this, an intense propaganda of a totalitarian type ensured a climate of permanent exaltation which could easily be used to frighten or neutralise the old, and until then decisive, political and labour machines, regardless of their leanings. In Argentina, the same day saw the burning by Peronist groups of the Jockey Club and of the headquarters of a socialist newspaper which housed a particularly rich collection of union literature. The concept of an independent union movement was at the same time, and in the name of the workers themselves, destroyed by the creation of an entirely new union framework. The new officials depended directly on the Ministry of Labour and the social security services, and their function was to ensure liaison between the centres of power and the workers' organisations. After the collapse of the Peronist régime and of Vargas's *Estado Novo*, the system of state-linked trade union officers continued in the context of a virtually unchanged framework of social legislation and, in most cases, without any change of personnel.

One can draw some conclusions from these changes within the working classes and their organisations (and the examples could equally well have been taken from Peru, where the labour federation is affiliated to APRA, or Mexico, where the various federations depend on the good will and protection of the presidency.) Except during the first stages of industrialisation, and then under the influence of immigrant activists, there has never been in Latin America a true working-class party. Apart from the anarcho-syndicalist federations of the turn of the century, the workers have given no sign of a desire to conquer society. In a minority when compared with the total population, with no special rôle in essentially agrarian countries, with no common origin or traditions, more frequently used than represented in politics, the working classes have either aided the rise to power of the middle classes or helped in the establishment of new political power machines.

With some exceptions, the 'integrationist' conception of the union movement is now admitted by the union leaders themselves, whatever their political opinions. Here again the result is a desire to influence state decisions and take part in public or semi-public administration. Thus, one finds the international organisations, and in particular the free federations—CISC and CLASC—multiplying schools, study groups, lectures and meetings for the formation of militants on the basis of European or American experiences, without the same effort being devoted to creating and developing union locals in factories and the services. Even before the organisation reaches maturity, the militant is replaced by the civil servant.

II

Challenges and Gambles

1. *The Imperatives of Change*

One cannot speak only of a pyramid, with the oligarchy at the apex, a population of serfs at the base, and the middle class connecting them and correctly describe these societies. This pyramid exists but it is only one of the forms taken by the social structure. There are other privileged groups and other methods of exploitation. The survival of the oligarchic system does not rule out the existence of different, more modern, relationships between heads of enterprises and wage-earners, any more than the functioning of specific mechanisms linking power groups and *clientelae*. Most Latin American countries cannot be described in terms of a single model of society: several models are applicable.

This coexistence or superimposition of social categories represents the survival of marginal archaic forms, the existence of more recent but congealed structures, and finally the appearance of new strata which reflect the moving sectors of a multiple society. It is precisely the absence of a ruling class—or the dynamism of a class aspiring to rule—and the equilibrium born of the traditionalism of groups deriving a meagre benefit from their common economic stagnation which gives these countries their original character. The rise of groups, the sharing of benefits, and aspirations for more—all take place and operate without any change in the existing situation, maintaining the

36

status quo as if fundamental upheavals frightened not only the privileged but also the candidates for the succession.

It becomes, however, impossible to maintain these various social structures and these multiple types of dependence, with no common principle or co-ordination, once internal processes and external influences provoke or demand change; once, that is, increasing sectors of the population can no longer accommodate an unchanging standard of living and inflexible institutions.

The first imperative of change is a demographic one. Not that Latin America is overpopulated relative to its resources: the 206 million people who were estimated to inhabit the continent in 1960 make up 10 per cent of the world's population, and occupy more than 20 per cent of the world's land area. As Kingsley Davis remarks, the natural resources of the continent are clearly superior to those of the main mother country, Spain; nevertheless the net product per capita is considerably less than that of Spain: $295 as compared with $324 in 1959. What is demographically significant is that, within a relatively unchanged social structure, the increase of production is meagre and slow, whereas that of population has since the 1920s been one of the highest in the world. In 1920, the population was 91 million. This rose by 1930 to 109 million, by 1940 to 131 million, by 1950 to 162 million, by 1960 to 206 million, and by 1970 it should have risen to 265 million.[1]

Australia and Argentina are geographically similar: they were colonised at the same period, their natural resources are comparable; but Australia's income per capita is two and a half times as high as that of Argentina.

Without entering into a discussion of the merits and defects of the theory which associates population increase with industrialisation, one should point out that the trends towards the increase in fertility rates and decrease in mortality rates, together with the consequent increase in population, are constant and lasting in Latin America, whereas the rise of the national product is largely dependent on factors external to Latin

37

America, notably the ability of world markets to absorb the supply of raw materials. To quote Kingsley Davis again: 'In 1954–59, the gross national product per capita increased at an annual rate of 1·3 per cent, but the rate of increase of population was 2·7 per cent per annum.'[2]

Despite variations from country to country, one should note that the increase in population is no longer due, as it was in certain periods, to massive immigration or to movements of the labour force, but corresponds to an increase in the birth rate. The exceptions are Argentina and Uruguay, the two countries which were colonised relatively recently.

Urbanisation and the concentration of the population—related to the demographic explosion—constitute the second challenge to the structural and institutional bric-à-brac accumulated by the Latin American past. There were, of course, large cities already—Buenos Aires, Rio de Janeiro, Mexico City—just as there were constant flows of internal migration following the traditional routes from the highlands to the coast and along the rivers. But the great migrations are recent, draining tens and hundreds of thousands of families from the *llano* and the *pampa* to the towns, from the *fundo* and the *hacienda* to the provincial or national capital, and to the outskirts of the metropolis where one squats and waits, hoping to enter a new life.

The fluidity of the population is a continental as well as a national phenomenon. It was once traditional for the adventurous youth of small towns in western Uruguay to follow the Paraná, from Salta to Santa Fé, and from Rosario to Buenos Aires. Human geography disregarded official frontiers and there were Paraguayans and Uruguayans in Buenos Aires who had never been to Montevideo or Asunción. Likewise, Chileans from the Cordillera visit Mendoza much more easily than Santiago. After the First World War, the adventure was no longer an individual or a group one. It became massive and collective. It was not so much the call of the city needing labour to industrialise as the rejection of labour by the rural areas. Between the 'refuse civilisation' of the slums and *ranchos* built around the cities and the hopeless slumber of the country, the choice is clear. It is a choice between certain social death and the possibility of social life. Economic development, the construction of factories and workshops and the need for labour bear no correspondence to the movement to the towns and capitals, but concentration continues. Rio de Janeiro, which had a population of 1·5 million in 1920, reached 2·3 in 1950; Greater Buenos Aires is congested with 8 million; Santiago, with varying degrees of comfort and overcrowding, houses 2 million out of a total population of 8 million; Mexico City has swollen to 4 million; and Caracas absorbs 100,000 new arrivals every year.

With the general population increase, the rural areas are not emptied. They are reservoirs that overflow. Paraguayans go to populate southern Brazil and northern Argentina; Chileans advance as far as Patagonia and the Atlantic coast (there are some 15-20,000 in Mar del Plata); Bolivians go down to the neighbouring Argentine provinces for the sugar-cane harvest or for periods of seasonal labour. Sizeable masses of people move, settle down, and then beg or demand.

According to the booms and recessions provoked by the fluctuations of raw material prices (rubber or coffee) or by rapid industrial growth, the Brazilian population increases or decreases from one region to another. In the ten years from 1940 to 1950, variations in the states of São Paulo, Minas Gerais, Paraná or Pernambuco affected millions of people, who followed two main currents: from decadent agricultural areas in the north-east to developing agricultural areas in the south and south-east, and from agricultural areas to the centres of industrial expansion, São Paulo and Rio de Janeiro.[3]

The social and political consequences of these migratory currents were considerable. The old oligarchic relationships of dependence were broken, and had to be replaced by new mechanisms. In the cities, masses of newcomers looked for the protection and security that become all the more necessary when the expansion of a certain type of industrial society cannot absorb and assimilate them. Once again, this time in the political field, we find the phenomenon of 'availability'.

When he abandons the traditional social structure and loses his old attitudes the individual or family head who is isolated in a mass of men in a similar situation becomes receptive to a new form of solidarity. The idea of a nation becomes comprehensible to him. The old institutions and ideologies based on outdated situations no longer mean anything to him. A new collective outlook, new formulas of organisation, and new ideals of a general kind are necessary to integrate him into a society which, by the mere fact of his presence in it, cannot resemble that of yesterday. Two new themes—'people' and 'nation'—have been added to the traditional vocabulary of propaganda, agitation and the struggle for power. Those who speak of 'people' and 'nation' frequently come to power, but it is not always the power of the people. Faced with the rapid and continuous rise in the number of inhabitants, coupled with the phenomenon of an urbanisation unrelated to the needs of industrialisation, which concentrates a fifth, or a quarter, or sometimes even a third of a country's population in a single city, the old social hierarchy and the institutions that maintained or concealed it could not but become out of date. In the rural areas the old society could still survive, but it was no longer *the* society.

A further factor—the declining rôle of Latin America as a producer of primary products for the rest of the world, and for Europe and the United States in particular—intervened and made change all the more necessary. The standard picture of a rich Latin America which could comfortably export its primary products, its cereals, its meat and other foodstuffs, and obtain in return manufactured goods and machinery from its highly industrialised customers, is no longer valid.

The picture corresponded to reality in 1913. In that year, Latin American exports to Europe totalled $963 million, and its imports from the continent—mainly from Britain, Germany and France—amounted to $793 million. At that time more than 25 per cent of the United States' imports came from Latin America, whose share of American exports was almost 14 per cent. The situation was characterised by intense trade between the southern countries of Latin America and Europe, whereas the United States had closer links with Central America, the Caribbean, Colombia and Venezuela.[4]

The First World War produced changes in the direction of trade. The European countries could no longer maintain the volume of their trade, and the United States became avid for clients. The post-war years saw an impoverished Europe attempting to recover its previous position, and a prosperous and expanding United States.

Concomitantly with the reduction in the volume of trade with Europe and the expansion of commerce between Latin America and the United States, the importance and nature of investments began to change. European capital was scarce, American capital abundant. Britain, faced with the victorious competition of the United States, withdrew to the safer markets of the Commonwealth. Australia, Canada and British possessions in Africa were to benefit from preferential treatment vis-à-vis the countries of Latin America. Those countries which had had traditional economic links with Europe—Argentina, Uruguay, Chile, Peru—attempted to renew them, with partial success. By virtue of its massive investments, however, its liberal credit policy, and its ever-increasing capacity to consume primary products, the United States was successful, particularly in the northern half of the continent. In the Caribbean it provided 60 per cent of all foreign investments; and Brazil was raised to the position of its third most important supplier and customer.

In 1929, the United States received half of Latin America's exports. The following year brought crisis and prices collapsed. Countries that imported raw materials and agricultural products reduced their purchases to a minimum. For the Latin American countries, trapped by their economic specialisation and deeply in debt, the effects of the depression were devastating. By 1931, they had reduced their imports to one quarter of what they had been two years earlier, and were attempting to maintain a meagre flow of goods by means of bilateral agreements. There were no immediate possibilities for industrialisation and product diversification. Consequently, the experiences of the depression produced a surge of nationalist ideas and plans, which from then on were to be part of the stock-in-trade of most political movements.

The aftermath of the crisis, the effects of the Second World War, the Korean War and East-West tension, increased the precariousness and fragility of the Latin American economies. Two new factors became important. There was a reduction of imports by the United States. In 1950–1959, 45 per cent of Latin American exports went to the United States; by 1961 the proportion had fallen to 38 per cent. The economic recovery of Western Europe redressed the balance to a certain extent, but the protectionist policies and preferential criteria established by the EEC restrained or prevented the re-establishment of flows of trade and their expansion as far as Latin America was concerned.

On a general level, technical progress has resulted in a relative abundance—in terms of trade, if not in terms of needs—of primary products. The Latin American economies are handicapped in the competition for markets in so far as they are insufficiently or not at all modernised as regards production methods and marketing efficiency. They are no longer the only, and the main, primary producers; they do not belong to any of the principal economic blocs; and they have not equipped themselves in terms of economic competitiveness.

The consequences of this situation go beyond trade figures: their significance lies in how they impinge on the inhabitants of the cities or the rural areas. There is a marked increase in internal consumption, not only of consumer goods, which have become indispensable for modern living, but also of food-stuffs. Time and again, the Argentine authorities have tried to limit internal meat consumption so as to have a surplus for export. In Uruguay, the increase in internal consumption— and the decline in the size of cattle herds—has threatened meat exports, which are the basis of the entire economy.

None of the classes or social strata is able to answer the count-less problems raised by these imperatives of change: neither the oligarchy, which prefers to draw in its horns and wait for better days when it feels threatened by events; nor the commercial bourgeoisie, which depends on situations it attempts to exploit but which are beyond its control; nor the industrial capitalists, dedicated to limited enterprise in times of crisis and mediocre self-sufficiency, now driven out of their markets by the power and efficiency of the industrial economies; nor the dispersed, closed and hopeless world of the rural areas; nor the working class, disorganised, small and non-conquering. There remains only the amalgam of the middle classes, which can provide not a class with a precise economic and social rôle, but pressures, ideas, and new administrative personnel.

According as these problems demand an immediate solution, and in the absence of any programme or plan, pressures, claims and hopes tend to cluster round the state. It is the state which, by trial and error, must search for an equilibrium between imports and exports, take measures to ensure monetary stability, draw up a credit policy and provide for housing. Its real power is limited by a treasury in the red, by the ebb and flow of interests and pressure groups, and by the need to maintain an inefficient administration staffed by political appointees. While reflecting in its functioning the societal contradictions which it must channel, fuse and complement, it develops and progressively becomes the main, if not the only, organiser of the nation. Functions which are not assumed by the privileged classes and not claimed by the working classes create a series of organisms with an entirely new social composition. Their rôle will be decisive.

The ideologies that accompany or justify this phenomenon vary according to fashion and chance, from positivism to Maoism, through a whole spectrum of varieties of socialism and fascism. Their effective influence is minimal. The true source of these ideologies is in the economic, social and political situation of each country, in the chaotic flux of populations which can no longer be contained and ordered by the archaic and elementary structures of the oligarchy, in the inability of each and every social sector to take, keep and use power and to face up to the problems of nations in the process of formation.

One should think neither of a state serving as the instrument of a class which organises, protects, administers and makes plans, nor of a state which functions according to theoretical frameworks copied from European or North American constitutions, but of a state which has taken on the functions of a political class. This is the only definition which fits the apparent confusion of events and convulsions in Latin America, and the only definition which permits one to discuss the same tendencies both in countries struggling to find an equilibrium and in those which have attempted to create a new structure by revolutionary means.

2. *The Student, Candidate for Power*

In the initial manifesto of the Reform movement, one finds a kind of 'Hymn to Youth': 'Youth lives ever in a state of heroism. It is disinterested. It is pure. It has not yet had time to be contaminated. It never makes mistakes in its choice of masters.' This adolescent idealism recurs frequently in the acts and writings of student youth. Ephemeral but renascent newspapers and bulletins, and student groups with significant names—*Crisol* ('Crucible'), *Inquietud* ('Restlessness'), *Brecha* ('Breach'), *Renovación* ('Renewal')—spontaneously maintain an attitude of rejection of what is, of protest against injustice and hypocrisy, of aspiration to possible social utopias. Each generation rediscovers the sordidness of society, and each generation is attracted by a new form of evasion. It is a misunderstanding to smile as if this were a passing, and hence inconsequent, phase and to justify one's smug scepticism by observing these same rebels indulging in and accepting, a few years later, the practices they once condemned. Some remain faithful to their youth and can be found today among the *guerrilleros* of Peru or Venezuela, or still harbour within themselves a longing for what they once believed in.

The post-1918 Reform movement in the universities was marked by two distinct but complementary features. On the one hand, it opposed the sclerosis and academicism of traditional forms of teaching; it wanted an autonomous, modern and open university: a university sensitive to the aspirations of the younger generation. At the same time, it saw the new university as the main instrument of social transformation on the national and continental scale. The scientific spirit, freedom of research, independence of thought: these were to create men suited to the times.

The movement left a deep impression on university and political life from one end of the continent to the other. It embodied the aspirations of intellectuals tied down and frustrated in their rôle by outdated institutions. The basic values put forward could gather together all the energies that could find no outlet in an archaic society: 'nationalism, anti-imperialism, populism and an anti-oligarchic attitude, secularism and anti-clericalism, pro-Americanism and anti-Europeanism, democracy and anti-totalitarianism'.[5] Half a century of struggles and experiences, together with changes in social structure and political institutions, were to transform the militant Reform movement into a tradition manipulated by new forces.

Once the universities had been reorganised and their previous slumbers had been replaced by frenetic activism—periods of internal unrest alternating with state-imposed discipline—an equilibrium was no longer possible between society and the educational system. Society was neither logical, nor rational, nor harmonious, and the universities could do nothing to reform it unaided.

Two consequences are apparent. Firstly, university reform stimulated the rise of several parties—nearly all the democratic parties, from APRA in Peru to the Partido de Liberación Nacional in Costa Rica—which attempted to do for society what the Reform movement had done for the universities. Secondly, the university, unable to harmonise with an immobile or slow-moving society, became a kind of society in itself, and sometimes a state within the state, with its own life, conflicts and problems, given grudging support by the authorities but restricted to the fringe of social life.

The student movements had aimed at being the motors of social transformation, but they have become partly schools for politicians, partly spheres of influence and recruitment for the political parties.

When one enters the old buildings of certain faculties of the University of Buenos Aires, whether groping for a professor's room, hidden by immense propaganda placards, or brushing against banners that hang from the ceiling and the window recesses and walking over a carpet of tracts and petitions, one has the unmistakable feeling of being somewhere which has no relation to teaching or to research, or even to students who hope, through their studies and university experience, to exert some influence on society. The place resembles, rather, a marketplace of ideas or a permanent electoral campaign. The watchwords have nothing to do with university problems, or even with national ones; only with China, Cuba, the Congo, Vietnam. The MUR attacks the MAR and forms a common front with the MOR in demanding that the political economy course devote more of its time to 'Marxist' experiences.

It is the same at the ancient University of San Marcos in Lima, where the *patios* house gatherings of APRA's 'buffaloes', of

Belaúnde's 'coyotes', of the pro-Chinese detachment, all waiting for the lecture which is to be supported or sabotaged. As for the University of Caracas—a 'free territory'—its gardens are patrolled by student guards and in the refectory the partisans of the illegal National Liberation Front greet the arrival of a *guerrillero* leader with a resounding '*Salud, comandante Pérez*'. The provincial note is sounded at Montevideo where the orator who harangues the crowd from a high stairway of the university frequently begins his speech with the formula, 'Once again we are masters of the streets.' In fact, that particular street (the widest of the central avenues), has for some hours been carefully closed to traffic by the municipal police so as to allow the 'revolutionaries' every facility for spreading their ideas.

If the picture of university life depicted only these tragi-comic scenes, it would clearly be a false one. Many students stand apart from political struggles, even if they follow them. In Buenos Aires, most students have to work to pay for their lodging, their food and their clothes. To the time spent attending lectures must be added the hours they spend working. And their long-term prospect is a degree and an underpaid job.

Student associations devote a good part of their energies to technical questions and university problems, thus fulfilling their rôle as corporate organisations. While the stage is occupied by the agitators and the mouthpieces of political groupings, student life continues and produces another type of student more interested in preparing for a professional career. There is also a certain tradition which is apolitical, or distrustful of politicians, which continues and which largely explains the rise or the success—in Buenos Aires, in Santiago de Chile, and in Caracas—of Christian Democrat groups who appear to care more for university life in the narrow sense of the term.

Nevertheless, it remains true that for aspiring politicians militancy in the university represents an excellent school for 'leadership'. Once the foot is in the stirrup, possibilities of a political career appear. In case of failure, one can always retreat into university posts such as teaching or administrative assistantships; or, as a makeshift, a boring career. If one could collect statistics of the number of ex-student leaders in political positions, one would doubtless find confirmed what direct observation leads one to suppose: namely, that the university militant is a natural candidate for the new ruling class.

3. *The Army as State and the Army as Party*

According to some social scientists, the army—or, more precisely, the armed forces—represents the middle class in an essential sector of the state's institutions. Others argue that since the basic function of the armed forces is to maintain order, they are simply an instrument of the privileged classes and above all of the oligarchy. The two interpretations are not necessarily contradictory if one regards them as relative and as appropriate to different periods and different situations.

An examination of some of the army's functions reveals that in addition to its purely military functions, it also performs civil and political rôles. The Argentine euphemism for the army—'a power factor'—does contain a measure of truth. One must remember that, in most Latin American countries, the army is the only nation-wide organisation, the only group which can act from the capital to any point on the frontier. Furthermore, the army is the public service least affected by changes in régime. A political crisis can produce a complete renewal of the administration, but the army would cease to exist if subjected to the same treatment. It is thus the one firm pillar of the state. Finally, for these reasons and as a consequence of its own constantly re-affirmed and proclaimed self-image, the army takes on the rôle of guardian and symbol of the nation.

Largely autonomous and endowed with a considerable budget and technically qualified personnel, the army tends naturally towards a kind of self-sufficiency. It attacks problems that are not dealt with on a national scale by civil governments, and establishes its own organisation in fields still virtually untouched by the civil service.

It is hard to generalise about 'the Latin American army' for here as elsewhere the situation varies greatly from one country to another. It is nevertheless significant that for several decades it was only the military schools that trained engineers and technicians in Brazil. The creation of a national steel industry in Córdoba was initiated by the Argentine army. For a long time the only complete communications networks in the continent— telephone, telegraph and radio—were those of the armed services, and the army was frequently the main or the only organisation involved in exploration, cartography and surveying. In the Andean regions, the army was the only national institution in permanent contact with the Indian population; and for Indian recruits it came to be the only representative of the modern state. Peru presents one of the clearest examples of this double rôle of the army. The unique position of the military in a country where, apart from APRA, there has never been a solid party framework on a national scale, makes it of fundamental importance.

The rise and fall of *caudillos* and political leaders whose popularity is based on opportunist promises or the propaganda of public works helps to give the army its rôle as arbiter. Without being a party or an administration, it can, should the need arise, by force of arms and by means of its own high level of organisation, assume the rôle or perform the functions of either.

There has been a continual evolution in the character and functions of the armed forces. The beginning of the nineteenth century was the age of the *caudillo*, and every intelligent and ambitious officer could nurse the hope of ending his career as president. The civil party—the representatives of the large landowners and mining interests—eventually imposed its own personnel on the state, but gave the army a part to play. Army officers were smothered with offices and titles, and the end result was an alliance to safeguard the privileges which were now common to them both.

49

At the professional level, a new class of officer engineers, geographers and explorers came into being whose members devoted their energies to building railroads or bridges. The rôle of the new officer was not as brilliant as that of the general who was an expert in rebellion or in court flattery, but he foreshadowed a figure whose importance was to grow as the complexity of social and economic problems made parades before powerless government officers superfluous and increased the importance of technical knowledge in the service of the state.

The birth of an industrial and commercial bourgeoisie and the increasing pressures brought to bear by the urban middle classes limited the influence of the traditional ruling class, whose interests were concentrated on exports, who were unconcerned with the social development of the country and whose automatic response to social tensions was the use of force. This change in the composition of society and in the classical comedy of apparent power was accompanied by the appearance of an urban proletariat and the slow but irresistible awakening of the hitherto marginal Indian population. Within the armed forces the new structure of the nation and the nature of the new problems to be faced produced a change of attitude, although the nature of this change varied according to seniority, the branch of the services, and social and regional origins. To achieve its rôle as arbiter and cease being the caste where 'the man on horseback'—needed by the civil authorities to maintain their control and impose their conservatism—was recruited, the army had to develop a policy.

The purely militant phase, with its purchase of expensive and useless foreign armaments, is over. Wars with neighbouring countries are now out of the question. The maintenance of order is insufficient, by itself, to inspire the younger generation of officers, which is sensitive to the spirit of its times and its social problems. Under these conditions, the rôle of the army is itself open to question. The Centre for Advanced Military Studies (CAEM), an institution created in Peru to prepare the military command for the needs of national defence, is rapidly becoming a centre for the study of social and economic problems. It puts forward one doctrine: 'The fundamental goal of the state being the welfare of the nation, and the armed forces being the instrument used by the state to implement its policy, *viz.* to ensure the collective well-being, the armed forces have as their mission the safeguarding of the social well-being, which is the supreme goal of the state.'

The conservative groups in Peru have reacted promptly to this claim to intervention or to participation in the conduct of public affairs. The army, and more particularly the CAEM, is accused of being influenced by extremist doctrines and of infiltration by communist sympathisers. Its great rival is nevertheless APRA, the party founded by Victor Raúl Haya de la Torre. It is the only party which possesses a nation-wide organisation, with bases in every region of the country, with centres within every stratum of the population, and running an enormous number of services, ranging from workers' canteens to industrial apprenticeship centres. It is virtually a state within the state, and that the army cannot brook. The army can tolerate, uphold or favour any particular policy provided that the military budget—between 18 per cent and 25 per cent of the national budget—is assured. It is prepared to form an alliance with any presidential candidate provided that he is not in a position to limit its prerogatives and does not attempt to build up a complete power structure. But the army cannot accept, let alone recognise, a party which would deprive it of its rôle as arbiter and eliminate it as a factor decisive for the future of the country.

One can explain this rivalry and hatred in terms of past events, in terms of different social origins or in terms of the different parts played by each in Peruvian political life at various times. The memory of those killed in the clash between the army and APRA in Trujillo, in 1932, is frequently invoked. The revolutionary origins of the party and the army's rôle as policeman for the

51

oligarchy are explanations of the rivalry that have some substance. On the other hand, I believe that today the main reason for the incompatibility between APRA and the army is the fact that these two organisations are both capable of taking power and are both conscious of the nature of their rival. It should be noted that this rivalry exists only in terms of the struggle for power and has no relation to social programmes or to contradictory political leanings.

Monographs or studies in depth of the armed forces—social composition, social functions, military functions—are still few and far between. One can thus only put forward a few hypotheses based on impressionistic data. When the systematic study of the armed forces begins to produce results, many elements of the conventional wisdom will have to be abandoned.

The frequent interventions by the armed forces in Argentina have given rise to a widely held belief that the army is implementing a 'military' policy. A close examination does not confirm this belief. The Argentine army is a relatively open social unit, whose origins and development were characterised by the presence, both in the ranks and among the officers, of a large proportion of men of urban and middle-class origin. It remains one of the state institutions where social mobility and pursuit of a career continue to be possible.

This does not mean that the Argentine army, a modern organisation, and thereby more efficient than its political and administrative counterparts, does not intervene in politics. On the contrary, in 1930, in 1943, in 1955, in 1962 and in 1963, its intervention was decisive. But in none of these situations did it pursue a goal of direct and long-term government. The army itself contains several factions and frequently behaves in the same way as do the parties, with no more doctrinal cohesion, no more of a clear view of the future and no more definite an economic or social programme than is displayed by the latter. In short, the army takes part in the struggle for power without claiming power entirely for itself, limiting itself to securing the key positions—until June 1966, at any rate.

In exchange, and in spite of declarations of principle, the Argentine political parties all end up by allying themselves with a faction within these same armed forces. This is emphasised by José Luis de Imaz, one of the few sociologists who has examined the problem.

'Not having any manifest function—there have not been any wars—the military apparatus of the armed forces has ended up being considered by all political groups as a potentially useful instrument for the attainment of their own objectives. In this way, recourse to the armed forces as a source of legitimisation—underlying all the explanations that are offered— has become a tacit rule of the Argentine political game. A rule that nobody invokes explicitly but which has ensured some advantage at least once to every political grouping. A rule that all would have to deny publicly but which in his heart of hearts no Argentine politician could repudiate, for at some time in the past twenty-five years he will have gone to knock at the door of the barracks.'[6]

4. *A Changing Church*

'The overwhelming majority of the population of Latin America is Catholic; I should be less assertive if I had to describe them as Christian.' This comment, made by a Roman Catholic priest, and raising the question of the responsibility of the hierarchy, is important, for it underlines a possible confusion between the appearances of spiritual power and the actual behaviour of the faithful.

In the poor districts of Bahia, one finds the ritual ceremonies of *candomblé*. The joyful, breathless and ecstatic participation of Negroes, mulattos and whites is entirely different from the atmosphere of a Catholic church service, but fixed to a wall can be seen a wooden Christ. Inscribed on it is the injunction, 'He should be respected.' This is, of course, a limiting case. One can interpret it either as a precaution against the religious authority of the Church or as a greeting addressed to a sympathetic Jesus who does not belong to the family.

In a high Peruvian valley, mass is said in Quechua. The acolyte sounds a sea-conch at the moment of elevation, and the *cholo* priest officiates to a crowd kneeling on the bare ground. Very different is the mass celebrated in the cathedral in Buenos Aires, where the elegant faithful, ladies in their hats and officers in gala uniform, meet as in a ceremony reserved for an élite. The Mexican peasant who turns to his saint to ask for aid or a favour and who thanks him with a votive painting* but who will strip the saint of clothing and ornaments if his request is not granted, does not, on the face of it, have the same conception of his faith as does the Chilean office worker who is militant in Catholic Action and who reads Maritain.

The Church hierarchy in Latin America is a human organisation and is not immune to history and to social conditions. A great deal of tolerance is necessary if it is to keep under its aegis the masses whose faith and religious practices are frequently near to heresy. On the other hand, discipline is all-important at the apex, at any rate when the power of the Church is undisputed and its authority is not threatened.

Originally subject to the Spanish crown and charged with limited tasks, the Church in Latin America has characteristically supported the civil authorities and the ruling classes in exchange for recognition of its privileges and official functions. The apparent omnipotence of the Church is a result of the constant presence of its highest dignitaries among the large landholders, the conservative rulers and the paternalistic oligarchs.

When the forces of change become evident, the hierarchy resists and supports the political groups that oppose the reforms.

---

* These votive offerings are so numerous that a vivid picture of social life can be seen on the walls of many chapels.

The Church did not play any part in popular movements or in the emergence of the middle classes; these social forces became imbued with a passionate anti-clericalism, and the Church could only reply by strengthening its links with those most anxious to preserve the old structures. But anti-clericalism was so strong that the separation between Church and State occurred in countries such as Brazil, Chile and Mexico, where the majority of the population continues to consider itself Catholic.

The composition of the clergy helps to explain the position of the Church. Local recruitment of clergy permitted social mobility, but within society as it was, with its written or unwritten laws of domination. The road opened to the recruit was one-way and led to direct or indirect participation in the system of exploitation. The large proportion of foreign priests reinforced the general trend towards collaboration with the ruling class, for by language and historical tradition the majority was Spanish, —and the Spanish Church is not remarkable for its enthusiastic espousal of reform movements.

Coming from all the various social groupings that were changing or coming into being, political, labour and communitarian initiatives played their part in transforming a society in which the Church became progressively more marginal and reduced to being a mere pressure group. Politically militant Catholics found no inspiration in the teachings or declarations of the Church when they took up a stand in regard to national or international problems, and frequently found themselves in opposition to the hierarchy and its conservative allies.

In Chile and Venezuela, the continual growth of new political organisations led by activists trained in traditional Catholic associations, but who had since become alienated from them as a result of differences about social and economic problems or the means of achieving social changes that they considered essential, came to influence the bishops and the whole of the hierarchy. In both these countries, the Church ceased to support the conservative parties—which nevertheless claimed to be Catholic—or to ally itself with them. Moreover, since the end of the war, many young European priests, interested more in participating in social conflicts than in immediate proselytising, have come to establish themselves in the cities, towns, and peasant areas of Latin America.

For the continent as a whole, the spirit of modernisation or adaptation seems to have come from outside, from the Vatican. But it would be naïve to think that the Vatican's interest in the transformations taking place in Latin America and in associating with these changes a thoroughgoing reform of the methods and activities of the Church would be enough to give Latin American Catholicism, both religious and lay, a sudden discipline and an immediate unity. There are too many vested interests and too many divergent outlooks for there to be any reality in the facile picture of an army of Catholics directed by clergymen-generals, remodelling Latin America according to the directives of the latest Council.

Given the degree of regional differences and of differences between individual situations, one can do no more than discuss a few trends and positions. Firstly, one should not forget that the clergy, without thereby being indifferent to social realities and perhaps in response to and as a safeguard against the release of social pressures, attaches primary importance to the creation and strengthening of communities of the faithful, thus fulfilling a mainly pastoral rôle. Secondly, one must take into account the ecclesiastical 'apparatus', whose elements cannot be changed or replaced without the intervention of a thousand local factors, but whose general orientation is nevertheless more sensitive to the influence of Rome. Finally, between the desire to create an entirely Christian society and the many ephemeral schools which cluster round ideas of Christian participation and presence in society as a whole, there are many points of disagreement and many divergences in outlook.

What remains clear, nevertheless, is that from being a static and condemned institution, the Church, not only that of the hierarchy but that of the faithful as well, has begun to move and is out to make new conquests.

5. *The State Technocrats*

A process similar to that which led to the formation of the managing élite of the Comissariat au Plan in France or in the European Economic Community is producing in Latin America nuclei or technicians, economists and planners. Their social origins, their training—through practical experience or in universities—and even their political affiliations are heterogeneous. They appear, meet and cluster as a result of a need felt at governmental level to come to terms with the social, economic and financial realities of the country, to foresee the immediate and mid-term future, and even to determine the approach to these problems and to help in coming to grips with them.

They are generally familiar with techniques of research and analysis developed in the highly industrialised countries. Their work or their research puts them in constant contact with European or American specialists. Thus, they have a first-hand knowledge of social structures, the mechanisms of production and investment, and of development. Whether they be 'national accountants' in Uruguay, ministerial experts in Argentina, directors of research centres in Venezuela or consultants to the state banks in Mexico, they have in common the fact of not belonging to the ruling oligarchic or bourgeois groups and the feeling that they form a new group with allied functions, placed near or within the 'corridors of power', but without any possibility of decision-making.

Another feature they have in common is their distrust of ideologies—but this does not rule out variations in their support of one political grouping or another. Some believe that the deadlocks reached on many different points by the existing ruling groups—which reflect the paralysing effect of the many countervailing forces brought to bear on the state—will eventually make their intervention necessary. Others believe that their future, or their possibilities of intervention, are linked to the nationalist movements which, under different labels and with the amorphous confusion of ideas and policies character- istic of great historical movements, provide the common de- nominator to all the forces of change. Some concentrate on the use to be made of the means which the outside world, with a variety of motives, is placing at the disposal of Latin American countries.

The common nature of their preoccupations and of their actual and potential rôles, in addition to the constant com- munication between them made necessary by the nature of their work, conditions them sufficiently for one to be able to see in them a potential ruling group. The allusion increasingly made to the '*cepalista* spirit'* corresponds both to a fear of a new force to be reckoned with—among the oligarchy and the traditional bourgeoisie as well as in political and military headquarters— and to a hope (among organisations favourably inclined to reforms) that all or part of this new management can be recruited to their cause.

To foresee whether they will become instruments or will con- stitute a new power is not easy and under present conditions would be closer to augury than to reasoned prediction. What is, however, certain, is that the high technocrats, whether as instruments or manipulators, will from now on be present in the evolution and in the revolutions of Latin America.

6. *The Class State and the State Class*

Most economic and social problems that cannot be solved by individual sectors of the population, whether privileged or dependent, require the intervention of the state. In the societies of Latin America, the state performs functions and takes on

* From CEPAL, the initials of the Spanish form of the organisation known in English as the United Nations Economic Commission for Latin America (ECLA).

forms that may seem similar to those of European states, but which turn out in fact to be quite different.

In these societies there have at all times been regional situations, caste or class systems, and commercial networks that have had only a loose relationship with the state, and which have led a kind of separate existence. One has perhaps to go back to the colonial period to find the roots of this situation. Even at this period, two systems co-existed: that of the power of the crown with its representatives and its services, and that of the local establishments (each with its own hierarchy and its own peculiar rules) to which the world of the Indians was completely marginal.

During the last decades many different types of state are identifiable. Between the rudimentary instrument for protecting the position of the dominant families and the state with decisive powers that has all the active sectors of the nation under its control, there are intermediary cases: a state made up of disparate elements, reflecting a society that is itself chaotic; or a state embracing two societies that cohabit in the same national territory but of which only one has rights and privileges.

This variety of forms suggests that one must abandon the naïve image of a state whose only functions are repression and administration for the oligarchy, a state which guarantees the status quo. It would be closer to the truth to say that the oligarchies' difficulties spring from the need to count on the support of the state.

The main point is that most of the changes undergone by the state imply an extension of its functions and field of action. The large landowners and exporters of minerals or foodstuffs conceived of the nation as a territory to be maintained like a hunting-ground, not as a people which could develop collectively. Wars and alliances with neighbours were waged or agreed for the sake of immediate interests and only rarely for the sake of the national interest. The army, the police, the magistrates, the teachers, the tax collectors and the customs officers were there because one could not do without them, and because *some* rules were necessary to avoid day-to-day friction and conflicts. Any changes were to affect only the façade, not the main structure of the edifice. The simplest solution was to copy the institutions of countries whose thought was old but whose power made them modern—so long, of course, as one did not carry out their provisions, or could entrust their interpretation, when matters became serious, to a sympathetic jurist.

The complexities of commerce, the consequences of distant wars, the arrival of foreigners bringing with them transforming techniques and ideas, the development of cramped populations within the old and simple structures and the growth of towns made it difficult and impracticable for the administration to continue being direct. Soon the oligarchy could no longer be sole ruler. When change overtook it, concessions had to be made and power had to be shared. But the new classes do not have the ambition, or the endurance, or the means to take power completely. Thence springs the peculiar rôle of the state: a rôle which, in the absence of a class able to impose its will and establish its own goals, was soon to become essential.

But here again, the Latin American spectrum is a wide one. It includes Stroessner's Paraguay, where the army, political life, administration, commerce and public works all depend, directly or indirectly, on the general-president of the Republic. In Chile, modernisation and industrialisation are the initiatives of public corporations; in Colombia, the state unifies a widely disparate nation. The spectrum also includes Mexico, where the relative size of the federal budget—over five times as large as that of the federated states put together—indicates the degree of *de facto* federation.

Two functions of the state are important both for their consequences and for an understanding of what really does happen in Latin America: property-ownership and entrepreneurship.

A study carried out in the early 1960s, with the purpose of

favouring the development of private enterprise, examined the ownership of the ten, twenty and thirty most important firms, respectively, in Argentina, Chile, Brazil, Colombia, Mexico and Venezuela. If one takes the data for the six countries as a whole, the following results emerge:[7]

Ownership	Top ten firms per cent	Top twenty firms per cent	Top thirty firms per cent
Latin American governments	78·2	68·1	62·4
Private sector (Latin American)	10·5	18·1	21·2
Private sector (foreign)	11·3	13·8	16·4
Total	100	100	100

A breakdown of the material reveals that the state owns or controls the following industries and services in each of the six countries:

Argentina: Oil, railways, iron and steel, banks, telephones, gas; part share in car and agricultural machinery production.
Brazil: Oil, railways, telephones, electricity, steel production, mines, credit banking.
Chile: Oil, railways, electricity, ports and docks, sugar, copper and nitrate; part share in steel and control over credit.
Colombia: Railways, public works, agricultural, industrial and mining credit, telephones and telegraphs, the merchant fleet, ports and docks, oil refining, electricity.
Mexico: Railways, electricity, oil, agricultural product distribution, credit banks; a large share in the steel industry.
Venezuela: Iron and steel, public works, chemicals, sugar, telephones, electricity, shipping, aviation and banks.

One should note that, in the list, oil is not included for Colombia and Venezuela. In Chile, on the other hand, copper and nitrate *are* included. It is clear that the inclusion or exclusion of these industries would have had a considerable effect in changing the proportions between the public sectors and the foreign private sector. Their ownership constitutes one of the key problems, at once social and economic, of the countries concerned. This alternative—ownership *either* by the public sector *or* by the foreign private sector—characterises the entire social and political situation in Latin America and limits the intervention of the domestic private sector. In other words, this alternative renders unlikely the possibility of a domestic private-enterprise economy as the outcome of present-day social changes.

It would be naïve to overlook the propagandistic nature of the study quoted. The Mexican Pablo González Casanova, using figures collected by his compatriot José Luis Ceceña, comes to slightly different conclusions as regards the rôle of the state.[8] Taking the one hundred most important enterprises, 50·27 per cent are owned entirely or in large part by foreign capital; 13·52 per cent by the domestic private sector; and 36·21 per cent by the state. What is important for our purposes, however, is the fact that González Casanova also believes that the Mexican public sector exerts considerable influence in the field of private investment and economic development, and that it occupies a strategic position as regards industry and the services. The extent to which the economic power of the state in Mexico is limited by the influx of foreign capital, by the credit policy of the United States, and by the volume of trade between the two countries, is an important problem, but a different one.

Likewise, the Mexican economist Víctor Urquidi believes that the state is in control of only a relatively small proportion of the total productive capital, 'even though in certain cases it monopolises particular industries and plays a considerable part in others'. He, too, assigns an essential rôle to the state, which can 'clearly intervene in the direction of private activity over a very wide front, without being either owner or entrepreneur, if it believes that economic development requires this intervention'.[9]

Raymond Vernon, who has written one of the best books on Mexico,[10] is prudent when it comes to conclusions or generalisations. But he is nevertheless clear when he describes the economic power of the state. 'The Mexican government has supreme control over three factors which are still scarce at this stage of Mexico's development, *viz*. credit, imports, and public services.' And he declares: 'The important fact is that the private sector operates in an environment where the public sector can launch a private firm or break its back.'

The absence of a ruling class able and willing to respond to all national problems, together with the consequences of geographical distance, and of exclusion from direct and continuous participation in the increasingly rapid development of the European and Anglo-American industrial centres, confer upon the state ever greater and more complex responsibilities.

The state, continually absorbing the so-called middle classes, becomes, in addition to its functions of national policy and defence, a machine called upon to solve, without any fixed doctrine but under the banner of different theories, the most diverse social and economic problems raised by a changing society. It cushions the pressure of sectors of the population who can find no outlet in the traditional oligarchic system by creating employment and by acting as a placement bureau for the most active members of the political parties. To compensate for the inertia of the ruling classes in the field of industrial development, it must become an entrepreneur. It resists the claims and the revolutionary pressures of the working classes by favouring certain categories of wage-earners and elaborating social legislation that makes it the arbiter of conflicts.

The multiplicity of its tasks and the contradictory nature of its activities—it is at one and the same time the guarantor of traditional forms of property and the creator of new sources of power—diversify its apparatus and differentiate the functions of its organs without there being any over-all discipline or orientation.

63

Latin American societies are made up of disunited castes, clans and classes. They are conglomerates, not communities; the strata that enter into their composition have their origins at different periods of time; they have not been eliminated or fused by evolution, they are juxtaposed. Hence the need for a permanent arbiter, be he president, *caudillo* or dictator. Hence, also, the difficulty of finding a system of rules and laws that would be acceptable to, applicable to and respected by the population as a whole.

Under these conditions, the state becomes the meeting-place where different social forces oppose each other, form alliances, or tolerate each other, there being no bond between them other than the fact that none on its own can rule. Simultaneously, it becomes the central power in the life of the nation, control over which means power not only over the administration but frequently over the decisive sectors of the economy as well.

The violence, passion and importance of political struggles become more comprehensible once one realises what the stakes are: virtually complete power over the institutions and the allocation of national resources. The maintenance of privileges, access to centres of decision, the availability of a large proportion of the national labour-force, the creation of new economic sectors, the control of credit, the manipulation of *clientelae*—all these derive in large part from political power.

Nevertheless, to attain this power and keep it is not easy, for the society is not one but many, made up of independent systems. Even dictatorial power can last only so long as it tolerates the maintenance of the advantages and way of life of one or another of the privileged groups.

Historical developments in Latin America have not only failed to destroy the old forms of society, but also, and more importantly, they have created a new society alongside the old. If the economic 'take-off' takes place and a new equilibrium is found, the 'available' masses will find employment and a function. Their desire to overturn will become a hope of integration. But economic conditions in most of the countries of Latin America are not favourable to the birth of a parallel society whose dynamism would condemn the old society to wither away, and so there appear formulas of total power and complete social renewal which tempt the younger generation. The idea is born that, from above and by force, power, in the hands of a new political class, could wipe out the past with all its contradictions.

III

Theories of the New Power

1. *In Search of the Party of Action*

If one is to grasp the true nature and rôle of the movements and parties that demand or provoke change, one must be wary of terminology. The observer finds it convenient to fall back on an established terminology when he is describing unknown actions and currents. As for the political leaders, presenting their programmes and methods as deriving from the great ideologies of the moment has its obvious attractions. This similarity of terminology has contributed greatly to misinformation about Latin America and to making the reality of events incomprehensible to international opinion.

The Bolivian Movimiento Nacionalista Revolucionario (MNR) is reputed to have been, originally, a party impregnated with German National Socialist ideas and under the influence of Nazi officer-instructors. This is of no use in understanding the deep social pressures to which the movement responded, the mentality of the intellectual groups who led it, or the solidarity with it expressed by other Latin American political movements with a good democratic record, such as Uruguayan Batllismo, Peruvian Aprismo, or Venezuela's Acción Democrática. It should be obvious that one must begin with an analysis of Bolivian society, with its white élite, its *mestizo* population aspiring to social mobility, its sizeable and newly awakening Indian population, its system of dependence centring on the mining barons, if one is to find the real forces behind the revolution in this country. Borrowings from distant ideologies, which are often fortuitous and may change with fashion, are of only relative interest. It would be equally wrong to try to understand Peronismo by detecting traces of Mussolinian or falangist propaganda in Perón's writings, rather than by examining the demographic, institutional and social factors that made the movement possible.

A salutary warning against simple explanations based on 'ideas' is provided by the victory in 1938 of the Chilean Popular Front with the support of the pro-Nazi leader González von Marées and of the ex-dictator Ibáñez. Another example, at the present time, is that of Clodomiro Almeyda, one of the leaders of the pro-Chinese faction in Chile. He was a supporter of Ibáñez and expressed sympathies for Peronismo; but it would be wrong to use these successive ideological affiliations to label Almeyda a political weathercock. His basic conception of a nationalist and centralist revolution has not changed.

Instead of attempting to classify every Latin American situation in terms of the imprecise categories of the European political and social context, one must try to extract from the varied vocabularies used by revolutionary, reformist or 'progressive' intellectuals what remains constant—despite their disconcerting propensity for changing parties and their fondness for the inspired imprecision of political oratory—in their behaviour and in their objectives.

The traditional political formations are characterised by the electoral machine. In the case of the conservative and liberal parties, these consist for the most part of electoral funds, a small number of militants and a large number of paid helpers at election time. The moderate parties that aim to gather together the middle classes and siphon off the urban working-class vote make more use of clubs and associations for the benefit of their political clients. Intense political activity coincides with presidential or parliamentary elections; between elections the leaders turn their attention to the distribution of the national budget.

The absence of a solid base at the grass-roots level and the tendency to focus their efforts on a few stable categories—civil servants, office workers, traditional workers' associations—put them at the mercy of the tidal wave unleashed by political *caudillos* or adventurer-demagogues. The danger increases as internal migration intensifies and upsets the traditional divisions of electoral geography. Trouble becomes inevitable when new problems outstrip, not only the normal financial resources of the state budget, but also the routine functioning of the public administration.

Despite their own peculiarities and variations in the national contexts, the Conservative and Radical parties of Argentina and Chile correspond quite closely to the above description. They are condemned either to radical transformation or to exclusion from political life.

Peru's APRA deserves a special study. It is remarkably organised and its many bases cover the whole of the national territory. Its central apparatus is strong and lively. It has firm roots among the middle class. It controls two leading trade-union federations, and is thus firmly implanted among the urban and agricultural proletariat. It is led by a gifted charismatic leader. Yet it has neither gained control of the state nor—as its organisation would have permitted—become a substitute for it. With the benefit of hindsight, one could perhaps find the reason in the indecision of its leader, Victor Raúl Haya de la Torre, whenever power was within his reach.

The fate of Venezuela's Acción Democrática has been entirely different. When the old oligarchic structures found themselves faced with the problems posed by oil and its royalties and crumbled under the weight of financial abundance, this party acted as a virtual substitute administration. The phenomenon is unusual since it was a case of mobilising the population, not to escape from misery, but to use and distribute the sudden and considerable wealth that was pouring into a society unprepared for it.

68

In no country is there a party better adapted to the conditions and requirements of the struggle for power imposed by recent developments, but one can discern some indicators that could herald the appearance of movements and tendencies whose still nebulous ends could become clearer in political crises.

If one examines the main themes exploited in the propaganda of the various groupings, and analyses what is constant in the changes advocated in the revolutionary and reformist literature, one can discern the ideas and ideals of a ruling political class in the process of formation. Its proponents may camouflage themselves with plumage borrowed from ideologies or doctrines originating in Peking, Rome or London, but this is not very important. What matters is their common rejection of the old forms of society: a rejection expressed in anti-feudal, anti-oligarchic or anti-imperialist slogans; in other words, the conviction that the social structure and the power mechanisms that derive from it must be completely remade. Essential, too, is their common conception of a nation yet to be created: a nation not as regards frontiers but as a solidary society, independent and controlling its material and human resources. They also share the conviction that the rôle of the state is decisive for achieving the two main aims of restructuring society: making it rational and efficient, and attaining full national sovereignty in relations with the outside world.

Less clearly stated, but present in nearly all these writings, manifestos and declarations, is the view that these primary tasks depend on the thought, the action and the decisive conquest of power of a new social class. This class is negatively defined by the rejection of the possible rôle of the other classes, by the critique of the natural limitations of the social categories called to join in building the new society, and by the importance that is repeatedly attached to the need for centralised planning, forecasting and direction—in fact, all of the tasks which the social groupings and institutions inherited from the past cannot pretend to be able to perform. From the contradictions, tensions and conflicts produced by the decomposition of archaic societies and the challenges of change there emerges irresistibly the prospect of a 'mission for a new class': a mission which, when closely associated with power, becomes extremely tempting to undertake. This prospect and this temptation are not theoretical in origin: they exist because of the vacuum created by the impotence of the other classes, the very nature of the problems to be solved and the importance of the rôle of the state.

But from this point on discussions and disagreements arise concerning the ways and means of attaining power, the forms of organisation which will ensure the cohesion of the new working class, and the techniques required to mobilise material and human resources for the creation of a national society. The important differences that mark the experiments that have already been made in Latin America—Mexico, Bolivia, Venezuela, Cuba—rule out pure and simple replication elsewhere, even though each of these triumphs of a new class was followed by a period of imitation, at least in the drawing up of political programmes and in the choice of a method of securing power.

This search by trial and error and these successive elaborations of strategic or tactical formulas are complicated by continual borrowings from European or American terminologies. The use of these terminologies sheds little light on events in Latin America, and serves but to confuse the issue. One doubts very much if reading articles translated from the *Monthly Review* really helps the intellectuals of Lima and Montevideo to understand their predicament. And when we find an Argentine Trotskyist group publishing a pamphlet demanding full power for the Peronist unions, it is surely reasonable to question the legitimacy of their intellectual paternity.

The main problem that haunts the 'available' intellectuals of the countries undergoing change is the choice of a method of taking possession of the levers of command, or, in more down-to-earth language, of participating in the responsibilities, perrogatives and advantages of power. Whether by elections or by violence, the new ruling class can only achieve power with the support of mass movements. An initial choice is made necessary, not on any theoretical grounds, but as a result of the concrete possibilities extant in the social and political situation of the country. The differentiation of tactical approaches, even when it takes a polemical or violent form, is a sign, not of a fundamental split within the class, but simply of disagreements between groups and factions of this class-in-the-making. They are disagreements about how to enter effectively into changing societies and about their own degree of 'availability' or integration. The student who fears that at the end of his studies no employment will be offered him at the level and with the privileges he feels are his right will be more disposed to choose the violent path than the professor or established engineer who maintains his place in society, for better or worse, by engaging in several paid activities. This divergence in opinion and choices of political method does not destroy the fundamental solidarity, based on their position in a changing social situation, that unites them.

With varying but generally undistinguished results, attempts have been made to found new parties, according to a modern conception of the party as an instrument of conquest, with a disciplined apparatus, centralised direction, the creation of specialised branches to correspond to the different sections of the population, the control of popular movements, the establishment of technical commissions to study national problems and the formation of ad hoc committees. The design of the machine is more often than not superior to its functioning, for on the one hand the headquarters themselves are made up of the débris of previous and rival organisations, while on the other the social groups to be harnessed are separate, compartmentalised or discouragingly fluid.

The Chilean Socialist party is a good example both of the desire to build such a machine for the conquest of power and of the difficulties faced by such an attempt. It would be sufficient to read the internal documents drawn up and circulated among its militants for one to be able to measure the difference between the theoretical model of Raúl Ampuero's organisation and the true state of the movement. The women's associations, the youth federations and the trade-union 'commandos' are not solidly aligned with the party, nor do they obey the instructions from the centre. The general secretariat succeeds in controlling congresses and most regular and statutory functions, but the party itself cannot mobilise, harness or manipulate the main sectors of the population. The weight of the past, the centrifugal effect of a collection of vested interests and the electoral tradition of political struggles, limit or paralyse the functioning of an apparatus conceived along Bolshevik lines.

Attempts to transform the old Social Democrat parties into centralised and well-structured organisations in Uruguay, Argentina and Mexico, have produced poor results. The language used is that of a militant and courageous mass movement; it reflects the spirit of those who use it, but it is not heard by those to whom it is addressed, and it ends up by isolating the spokesman of the masses from the masses themselves.

The Catholic Church, in its effort to participate in social life, is also trying to reform itself at different levels and by different means. From one end of the continent to the other, functioning centres for study or action are found. Whatever the immediate results, and the mixed fortunes that are the lot of every human experiment, the fact that these attempts are the result of international initiatives or are organised by the hierarchy assures them of permanence and renewal. The result is both an impressive accumulation of knowledge and practical experience and at the same time the formation of ever more numerous teams of specialists and militant social workers. Nevertheless, even in cases where the programme is oriented towards urban and rural unions, it is not among the worker or peasant populations that volunteer activists arise, but among intellectuals, students, petty bourgeois and white-collar workers. These make up the bulk of the Catholic Action activists and the leading groups of the Christian Democrat parties. The clearest successes are to be found in Chile and Venezuela, where the national factors of social and political evolution were determinant. Elsewhere—in Peru, Bolivia, Argentina, Uruguay and Colombia—the influence of the Christian Democrats remains marginal and experimental.

The victory of the Chilean Christian Democrat party in the municipal elections of 1963, in the presidential elections of September 1964 and in the legislative elections of March 1965, is the culmination of a long struggle which has lasted for about thirty years. Its successes and setbacks are closely connected with the social and political life of the country. The Conservative Youth (Juventud Conservadora, the movement's original name, or the Falange Nacional as it called itself after breaking with the Conservatives) and finally the Christian Democrat party were never absent from the significant events in the political development of the country. The fact that the movement was almost always in opposition, both in terms of the political struggle and in terms of policy, meant that its militants were immune to the temptations of apparent power and set their sights on real power. The extent and gravity of Chile's social and economic problems—problems that grew more urgent as the capital's population became more swollen and as the rural masses began to stir—revealed the incompetence of the traditional parties. The Christian Democrat movement possessed the required qualities—a new, competent, reforming and nationalist apparatus—to step into the vacuum.

In Venezuela, Copei, after a period of collaboration with the ruling Acción Democrática, has stepped aside and is waiting for the ruling party to lose its impetus and the confidence of the younger generation. As for the rest, one cannot compare the Chilean and Venezuelan situations without taking into account all the differences of national product, parliamentary tradition and geographical situation that separate them. The similarity lies only in the formation and functioning of the two Christian Democrat parties and their related social rôles.

2. *Three Convergent Solutions*

For the tens of thousands of 'available' Latin American intellectuals seeking a rôle to play, the choice of solutions and methods is wide and difficult. In the absence of an ideal type of organisation or of a technique for the conquest of power which could be easily adapted to the conditions of their country, a number of them adopt a pragmatic attitude, attempt to establish an inventory of the material available in the existing society which could be used in the construction of a new society, and decide to concentrate their efforts in the most promising direction.

An examination of the writings representative of some of the most conscious partisans of change can help to define what, beyond political or sectarian considerations, constitutes the common capital of the new class. From the vast, continuously growing literature, one must leave out of account that which only reproduces international propaganda in order to concentrate on the more significant production of intellectuals who face specific Latin-American problems. We shall therefore examine three different books: a nationalist essay, a Christian-social *prise de conscience*, and a Socialist interpretation.

The Brazilian sociologist Hélio Jaguaribe is an impressive example of a student who is fascinated by the complexity of his own country's social phenomena. To capture their changing essence, he uses methods and techniques derived from all schools of thought, without allowing himself to be hemmed in by any ideological system or doctrine. He has summed up in a few tightly-packed chapters his nationalist conception of the social and economic development of Brazil.[1] As for the idea of a nation, Jaguaribe considers it to be a dialectical process 'in which there intervene, as objective conditions that make it possible and motivate it, certain historical, social and geographical factors, but which only come into being by virtue of a project of national integration'. He distinguishes between a 'historically possible nationality, experienced as necessary by its members, but not yet constituted or consolidated politically' and nationality as a 'project for overcoming an obstacle which takes shape within the framework of a nation in being and already endowed with experience of life as a nation, but which can no longer exist within its traditional framework'. In other words, he distinguishes between an integrating nationalism and an imperialist nationalism.

Leaving aside the question of definitions, let us examine more closely the process as he describes it. 'The historical nation precedes and conditions the possibility of the political, voluntaristic nation.' A second factor, essential for the formation of a national community and without which one could have only a city-state or a tribe, is the political decision which replaces neighbourhood relationships with relationships of co-optation. This decision corresponds to 'the need felt by a collectivity, in a given situation, to ensure its social and economic development by means of the organisation and consolidation of the adequate institutional machinery'.

As far as Brazil is concerned, Jaguaribe believes that independence (1822) and the proclamation of the republic (1889) only added superstructural institutions to a past marked by a colonial and semi-colonial economy without bringing about any fundamental change. It was only after the creation of an internal market and, as a function of this market, of the preliminary phases of industrialisation, that a nationalist conception of the country became manifest. The First World War and the crisis of 1929 imposed an economic and social transformation which, taking place haphazardly, without plan or programme, provoked considerable inter-regional differentiation and gave rise to the need for integrating the country as a whole. From the 1930s, and more vigorously during the 1940s, nationalist feelings expressed themselves in cultural, economic and political fields.

The nationalist thrust, according to Jaguaribe, is inseparable from a trend towards greater participation in political life on the part of the masses, from a democratisation of institutions and from a greater autonomy in international affairs. Until this trend appeared, the ruling classes thought and acted, not with reference to Brazil, but as the instruments of the foreign industrial economies, and the working masses could neither organise nor stake claims since their incomes depended on a system of production for which prices were fixed abroad. The social forces which were to contribute to the development of the nationalist movement were thus the dynamic industrial bourgeoisie, the proletariat (which began to realise that its standard of living depended on the level of industrialisation), and 'the technical and administrative cadres and the middle-class intelligentsia, involved simultaneously in the process of development and in the internal and external consolidation of the state'. On the other hand, the 'cosmopolitan' element was swollen by the agrarian and commercial bourgeoisie and by a large section of the middle class: the tertiary sector that formed a parasitical and functionless cyst within the state.

Most of the problems faced by the country derive from the contradictions caused by the heterogeneity of society: under-capitalisation together with a distrust of foreign capital; under-consumption together with the need to build up a national capital stock; cheap but inefficient public services; the protection and consequent mediocrity of national industry; workers' struggles directed towards the establishment of a privileged corporate status; the state as a manipulator of electoral *clientelae*, and a budget with a growing deficit; a native culture coexisting with an imported culture; an official anticolonialist policy and, at the same time, alliances with European colonial powers; and so on.

Jaguaribe sees in nationalism nothing more than a pragmatic

ideology, a means for the attainment of the fundamental goal of development. It is not as a matter of principle that one should reject the exploitation of Brazilian oil by Standard Oil and choose nationalisation; it is simply that Petrobrás, in the present international situation and given the needs of the Brazilian economy, provides the best solution. Nationalism corresponds to existing problems; it does not exclude, at later stages, and when the grouping together and co-ordination of forces has taken place, participation in regional schemes; nor does it rule out supranational formulas. Social conflicts themselves are not, in the present situation, fundamental class struggles, but tensions between dynamic or static social structures. The solutions are given neither by capitalism nor by a Marxist formula— these being the theoretical expressions of particular phenomena and of particular periods—but by the need to integrate a community *politically*, by the need to keep its over-all problems continually in sight.

This flexibility in the choice of means and techniques—the goal being given in a precise manner—stands, not for indifference, but, on the contrary, for research. The industrial bourgeoisie can still lead the working and middle classes in the drive toward economic transformation. It can only do so, however, if its members act as spirited entrepreneurs conscious of their social rôle, and only if they resist both the backward sections of their own class and the backward-looking interests of the other classes. Nationalism is the alliance of progressive groups aware of the limits and possibilities of a given situation. If the bourgeoisie do not take their historic opportunity, the Brazilian community will choose the Socialist road.

What is important for a nationalist such as Jaguaribe is not the theoretical superiority of capitalism or of Socialism but the practical usefulness of either as a strategy for development. One indication of the instrumental nature of the discussions concerning the relative values of the two systems is the fact that, once development has been achieved, the two types of society

77

would tend to converge and the question of the nature of property would no longer be relevant.

This sketch of a nationalist programme does not, however, imply that the Brazilian economy should attempt to reach its maximum development within the framework of the present international division of labour. On the contrary, all the nation's resources should be mobilised and exploited so as to make possible a restructuring of this division of labour and give Brazil a new and more important rôle in the structure of international production.

From this analysis and this desire for change there follows a series of practical consequences all implying the reform of socio-economic structures and the search for the highest possible rate of capitalist accumulation. Solutions are sought neither in terms of good or evil nor in terms of the class struggle. The good capitalist is he who disengages himself from the colonialist past and performs his rôle as entrepreneur; the good member of the middle class is he who takes part in the efficient administration of the public services or of the enterprise; the good worker is he who relates his claims to increasing productivity.

If we now turn to what, while not explicitly stated, is nevertheless apparent in Jaguaribe's thinking, we note that the key idea underlying his argument is the need for the creation of a new state apparatus, no longer representing the de facto privileged groups and their clients but the whole community and able to bring its influence to bear on the future of the community as a whole. The industrial bourgeois, the petty bourgeois civil servant or 'cadre' and the productive worker are no more than elements in a solidary whole whose support and manager is the state. Political power is no longer an instrument but a force in itself. And if the model entrepreneur, in Jaguaribe's description, so closely resembles the administrator of the public services or the responsible civil servant, the explanation lies in the related rôles he outlines for them.

Moved by other preoccupations but facing comparable situations, Catholic intellectuals attach considerable importance to the phenomena of disintegration which underlie, for them, the absence of a true social order and contribute to the hypertrophy of the state.[2]

The main problem is for them the restructuring of society and the construction of a true national community. A short work by Julio Silva Solar and Jacques Chonchol—very general but representative of the thought of Christian Democrat thinkers and militants—presents a picture of an underdeveloped Latin America and outlines a possible development policy.[3] More than half of the book is devoted to a critique of the capitalist system of property, a critique backed up with quotations from Catholic priests and thinkers, with the aim of insisting on the Christian nature of the concept of a communitarian system. The argument is in no way peculiar to Latin America and seems to conform more closely to conclusions drawn from the experience of industrial societies. The transition between the general argument aimed at proving that Christian thought is not indissolubly tied to the system of private property (providing, in fact, a serious basis for the communitarian ideal) and the need for an examination of Latin American problems, is effected by the authors' remark that 'the positive reasons in favour of the new communitarian structure are to be sought not in the Bible nor in any other document, but in the objective examination of social and historical reality'. The first half of the argument appears to be intended to disarm the upholders of conservative Catholicism, traditionally linked, in Latin America, to right-wing parties, or at least to deny them the right of being the exclusive interpreters of orthodoxy.

For Silva Solar and Chonchol, Latin America is part of the underdeveloped world, for the same reasons as is most of Africa and Asia. Nationalism is a phenomenon common to them, and independence poses identical problems to their leaders: those of development, the reform of economic structures hitherto conditioned by production for the mother-countries, and the creation of an internal market and of progress which benefits the greatest possible number.

The most characteristic feature of Latin American societies is their high degree of social stratification. In virtually no country does there exist 'a true national integration of the various social classes'. Furthermore, 'social differentiation is so accentuated that in most cases it constitutes a virtual closed caste system'. The other characteristics are, on the one hand, a certain nationalist isolation that makes of the countries of Latin America 'unconnected satellites that orbit around the great dominant economies'; and, on the other hand, political instability, a constant oscillation between 'oligarchic democracy' and 'personal dictatorships of a more or less military hue'.

Following this analysis, the authors attempt to formulate a policy 'that would permit the overcoming, in the shortest possible period of time, of the conditions of underdevelopment' which is the fundamental task of every group that 'aspires in a responsible way to the conquest of power'. On the national scale, the reality and the nature of the problems faced vary from country to country, but the four main goals to be attained are the same for all. These are: the planning of development; the structural reforms that are necessary if development is to be made possible; national and Latin American economic integration; and, finally, the progressive achievement of democracy.

What is characteristic of the thought of the 'social Christians' is an explicit distrust of the dangers of *étatisme* and a particular importance attached to the possibilities of a common Latin American policy. Furthermore, their concentration on the practical and positive aspects of the problems to be solved compels them to admit that 'it would be utopian to deny that at the beginning the state will become hypertrophied'. They believe, however, that according as the new régime becomes organised, the functions of the state will be taken over by organisations of direct control on the part of the different sectors of the population.

They are aware of the contradiction between the need for rapid capital accumulation in order to make development possible and the desire to avoid any type of dictatorship or totalitarian system. They think, however, that it can be overcome by means of a kind of voluntary collective mobilisation: 'The only way of reconciling the accelerated development of a backward country and the existence of an institutional political régime is to create a great internal mystique oriented towards development and accompanied by properly conceived international aid on the part of the industrialised countries.'

An analysis of the concrete measures that the authors propose reveals (despite the fact that they do not approach the problem from this particular point of view) an ideal of a 'new man' and a new class corresponding to the goals they set and the functioning of the social system they propose. The structural reforms in the political and administrative fields comprise: a change in the articles of the constitution that grant excessive protection to individual property rights; a widening of the electoral base in order to give the means of political expression to the greatest possible number; the restructuring of the state administration so as to destroy its character as an employment bureau for political clients and make it instrumental; and the participation of representatives of all the main interest groups—trade unions, co-operatives, professional and regional associations—in the tasks of planning. Likewise, they propose that relations with the outside world be organised, not (as hitherto) on the basis of individual countries, but by means of an organisation assembling the twenty Latin American republics. The interests of Latin America would thus be represented for what they are and no longer be submerged in the present Organization of American States which, in view of the overwhelming superiority in all respects of the North American partner, is no more than a Colonial Office for the United States.

The economic reforms—agrarian reform, reform of enterprises —are characterised by the idea that the 'national community' will be the result of a series of state interventions, initiatives and adjudications.

> The production and distribution of all goods and services essential for the proper functioning of society, and which by their very nature should not be produced and distributed according to the criterion of private economic profitability but according to the criterion of general profitability for the community as a whole, should take place by means of state enterprises. State enterprises should likewise control the production and distribution of those goods and services which confer on those who control them power such as to cause potential disruption in the normal prosecution of the social goals of the community. Within this category fall, for example, banking, insurance, public services and the primary goods essential to the country's economy.

The authors do not neglect to insist that the participation of the population as a whole, its groupings and associations, at all levels and in all fields, will confer on the mechanisms of the state a democratic character. One should, however, note that this point of view implies the creation of an ad hoc social stratum composed of managers, administrators and civil servants. There is no way of telling beforehand whether this will become an example of 'corporativism' or of self-management.

The Argentine sociologist Torcuato di Tella examines the situation of his country from a Socialist point of view.[4] He determines the existing structure and observes the major trends in an attempt to define a possible policy. A 'Fabian' spirit is discernible in the book, and the depth of the author's knowledge permits him to avoid the romantic schematicism that is all too often characteristic of social theories in Latin America. Armed with study and comparisons, if not with direct experience, di Tella puts forward opinions and hypotheses that are generally not found in propagandist literature. Thus, he recognises that tensions and social struggles do not disappear in the 'Socialist' countries, and he admits the importance of the time-factor in social change, whether this be achieved by reforms or by revolution.

He first defines Socialist values in the broad sense, without attaching them to any school or tradition, and adding as well certain Christian ideals. All concern the human person: individual rights; opportunities for initiative; freedom in social relationships; a social system offering equality in the use of material goods; and participation in public and economic life by means of voluntary organisations. These permanent goals are those of a Socialist society. A series of obstacles, peculiar to the existing type of society and its trends, faces those who try to attain them. These obstacles are the result of structural limitations. The trend towards stratification is opposed to the egalitarian ideal; the need for centralised and bureaucratic state production contradicts the hope of greater autonomy; the concentration of power provokes on the one hand a need to create countervailing forces against the state, but on the other hand it accompanies the extension of public property without which no liberty is possible. The development of the existing society makes these phenomena inevitable, and a realistic Socialist policy must resign itself to them, adapt itself to them and, without forgetting the final aims, make a choice from among the multiple possibilities offered by the evolution of society.

The hierarchy of functions is a consequence of modern productive techniques; one should not, therefore, oppose these techniques but strive to avoid the establishment of a corresponding hierarchy of incomes. The Socialist policy would thus invoke the egalitarian principle, and, while recognising the functional necessity of the hierarchy, attempt to reduce income differentials. In some cases, however, di Tella argues, 'where the correct performance of these functions [management and specialised technical staff] is hampered by inadequate pay, as is the case for many management positions in Argentina, a Socialist policy should tend to increase the reward even if this implies greater inequality in the corresponding sector'.

The same productive techniques require the existence of large organisations, private or state-owned, to manage the economy and co-ordinate political functions. The inevitable existence of a centralising state endowed with wide powers over the economy, education and the police function implies the abandonment of the conception according to which Socialism would be 'an aggregate of autonomous organisations composed of individuals organised for production and other activities'. The ideal of decentralisation remains valid, as does that of the organisation of activities at the closest possible level to the individual, but for the time being it is only possible to favour systems that approach the ideal. Its realisation is at present unfeasible.

Purely political controls, no more than certain forms of administrative decentralisation for the management of large enterprises or the functioning of co-operatives, are not sufficient to prevent a dangerous concentration of power. The state must be able to plan the economy and impose the measures determined by the popular will, but one must search for alternative forms of public management of the economy—apart from private property—such as state corporations and municipal or provincial enterprises, in order to 'fragment' the economic power of the state without endangering the general purpose of the transformation.

Di Tella does not believe that labour unions provide an answer, particularly when nearly all the forces of production are in the hands of the centralised state. Furthermore, he does not think that union action provides sufficient protection for the individual against the abuses of his administrative superiors, particularly 'in the middle and higher ranges of the occupational ladder'. It is rather in voluntary organisations which seek to inform and educate public opinion, and in the organisations that administer certain social services, that the counterpoise to the all-powerful state is to be sought.

Returning to the elements that compose Argentine society today, di Tella describes the main mechanisms of change that could lead to Socialism. He sees five main factors as instrumental to this purpose: the economic organisation of the working class; the various popular and middle-class associations; groups of intellectuals who develop Socialist theory; Socialist professionals and technicians within the industrial and state organisations; and the political party 'as a force integrating and federating the sectors involved in the other four mechanisms, under specialised and in part professional direction'.

It is interesting to note that the first factor, the unions, is immediately afterwards discussed as being 'the principal source of finance for political movements based on the working class'. Their bureaucratic character and the relative alienation of the trade-union militants from the 'base' do not seem to present any dangers, for they can be corrected by a 'good system of internal communications' and by the presence of 'militant groups' who act as catalysts. The second group, that of the popular associations, is considered suitable to train the future administrative personnel of the various Socialist institutions, such as trade unions, parties, co-operatives and industrial workers' councils. It is, as the author puts it, 'a recruiting-ground for leaders'.

As for the intellectuals, it is their responsibility 'to bring political theory continually into line with the realities of the social environment'. Their influence cannot be immediate but can be brought to bear on public opinion by means of their studies, publications and newspapers and by a means—to be elaborated and modified according to circumstances—of liaison between intellectual associations and the political movement.

Socialist technicians and professionals can play a strategic rôle by virtue of their membership of a social sector which holds the levers of command over society and of the fact that they develop the technical norms according to which society is governed.

Finally, the political party gathers together the leading groups of the categories enumerated above in order to federate and articulate the forces favourable to change and decide the ways and means to be used to bring about this change.

The programme of measures to be proposed and carried out by a popular Socialist movement on attaining or on sharing power comprises, in its essentials, the nationalisation of public services and of the sources of energy and raw materials, the transfer to the public sector of the large corporations, state control over foreign trade, agrarian reform, the reorganisation of public administration, the planning of the economy, and the definition of a foreign policy independent of the great world blocs.

Time and again, the author insists on the importance he attaches to the participation, in the relevant sectors, of popular associations, and on the mixed and autonomous character that can be taken on by certain kinds of enterprises operating in the public sector. Nevertheless, the main argument of the book is characterised by the idea of a political headquarters aiming at and achieving the conquest of power, the functions of responsibility and control falling to a managerial class whose members exist within the present industrial and administrative framework and whose would-be successors can easily be seen in the bureaucracies that manipulate the mass organisations. Despite his references to the interests of the working class, it is not the labour unions or the co-operatives or the natural workers' associations who will be called upon to serve as basic cells for the construction of a Socialist society or to determine the tactics and strategy of social struggles. If one looks behind the invocations of Socialist ideals one finds a desire and hope for a new class which will be able to direct a changing society.

3. *The Relationship*

One should note that, in these nationalist, Christian-social and Socialist theses, a large number of the interpretations, goals and methods are closely related. But does this mean that they reflect the will of a class? This is tricky and uncharted ground, and one can only describe it by means of historical and cross-cultural comparisons. What one can say is that the elements of a managerial class, in the political, administrative and economic spheres, do exist. Furthermore, in view of the bankruptcy of the old oligarchy and the extreme feebleness of the industrial bourgeoisie, this new class could seize power. Finally—and this adds force to the argument—the prominent rôle of the state is favourable to, and to some extent shapes, the possible rôle of this class.

The easily discernible general trend in a series of situations and processes does not exclude the existence of contradictions or eliminate the diversity of possible choices within these composite intellectual groups themselves. These groups are now at different levels or performing fragmentary functions in a society which acts on them at the same time as they act on it. One cannot thus expect that the more clearsighted among them will develop the notion of a 'historic mission' which would mobilise all the other potential beneficiaries.

The famous 'middle class' which increasingly produces groups of beneficiaries, participants and conquerors in power, is full of tensions and conflicts. It is not easy to distinguish those who derive sufficient benefits from the status quo to become its defenders from those who, in a lucid or spontaneous way, foresee or desire new social structures of which they would become masters. What separates them out is the fact that the status quo is threatened by the nature and gravity of the new problems.

The broad outlines of an attitude take shape as a result not only of the theoreticians' search for a formula but also of actual experiences which accumulate finally into an inheritance of concepts and hopes to which all lay claim.

The Mexican system, which follows the formula of the

Partido Revolucionario Institucional, represents, for most of
the intellectual proponents of change, an example of what
might be. This régime gives to a new class the rôle of ruling and
of exercising power, not, as in Europe, at the end of a long
process, but as a prelude to the transformation and economic
development of the country. The adjective *revolucionario* is not
retained out of pious fidelity to folklore. It really does describe
the elimination of previous structures as regards the new men
of power and it underlines the determination not to return to
the old mechanisms. The selection and promotion of the new
rulers, the process of upward mobility for political or administrative groups, are carried out within and by the party following
written and unwritten rules that have emerged as a result of
continuous experimentation. Conflicts of interest and disagreements about the social and political future of the country are
fought out within the system itself. All the members of the
undeclared guild of those who hold power are agreed on the
common law of power. Indian problems, the agrarian question,
international politics and the rate of economic growth—these
are technical problems to be solved by the party-state apparatus.
All criticisms, demands and social movements, if they are to be
taken into consideration, must begin by renouncing any revolutionary aims, for no class in power will allow its function to be
questioned. The revolution is complete.

The most violent conflicts, whether they are expressed in the
course of struggles for power or emerge between groups which,
in power, disagree over means or tactics, are unable to wipe out
the social kinship that unites them. Today's opponent, in
prison or in exile, remains tomorrow's potential ally. The
Mexican extremist does not go so far as to refuse to serve the
régime or be protected by it. Similarly, in Venezuela, relations
between young revolutionary intellectuals and high government officials are never completely broken off. To the usual
explanations—social origin, generational solidarity, previous
political alliances, memories of university days—one must add

a reason that is seldom expressed but which carries weight in these groups and is connected to the traditional forms of power in Latin America: the tissue of kinship and friendship.

One entirely new social segment, consisting of engineers, technicians and the scientifically trained professionals, encounters large obstacles to its amalgamation with the new political class. This group cannot intervene except via a political grouping or, as is the case with its most able members, as representatives of international organisations, such as the international and Latin American financial or credit centres and economic organisations. Here again the nature of the problems to be faced gives them their best chance of incorporating themselves into the groups that control the structures that are being formed. They sometimes cluster round a given party or make up a political school; but, as far as the strategic options are concerned, it is hard to tell who, whether the Chilean economist of ECLA or the Argentinian engineer, is a Socialist or a Christian Democrat, a *gorila** or a *justicialista*.

So long as there remains a certain equilibrium or even a possibility of postponing change, in the bizarre social structures of Latin America the 'power groups'—whether they belong to the condemned past, to the transitory present or to the uncertain future—coexist and limit themselves to claiming their meagre or abundant share of the national budget. But if an economic crisis, or the strong pressure of new populations or direct foreign intervention destroy this precarious stability, the possibilities of evolution and adaptation of the institutional framework become too limited to answer the challenge and

*Gorila: a term originating in Argentina and now used throughout the continent (by the opposition) to refer to the partisans of strong-armed military government. It apparently originated in a satirical radio programme in which insolubly complex situations were resolved by the 'gorillas' whose philistine roarings and recourse to force as the ultimate means of dealing with *any* problem are the more precise connotations of the term when used in a political context. (See Carlos del Peral, *Manual del gorila,* Jorge Álvarez Ed., Buenos Aires 1964; and Horácio Daniel Rodriguez, "¿O que é um Gorila?", *Cadernos Brasileiros* VIII, 6, 1966, pp. 104 ff.)

ensure a return to equilibrium. The old oligarchical tactic of waiting for the storm to subside is now definitely outdated. Solutions *must* be found and the way is then open for a stake to be claimed both by those of the old 'power groups' such as the armed forces, which had previously been no more than instruments, and also by the new 'power groups' which, not yet endowed with a clear structure or a definite programme, can manifest themselves only via the power of the state.

In such a situation, one can observe the behaviour and aims of the various elements of the new class, as they suddenly become conscious of what their social possibilities are, as they face the residue of the old structures and the constitutional formation. In such a situation, too, these arise the temptations of the 'direct solution': the straightforward taking of power which would allow a return, on the following day, to the past which would then become a subject of discussion and no longer be a yoke to be carried.

The army, too, is faced with new possibilities and is torn between its allegiances and its impulses. It is the instrument of the state, but the state no longer functions and the army cannot replace it. It is tempted by power but is conscious of its limitations. It is faithful to its view of the nation but despairs of ever seeing the nation come into being. It is frequently willing to govern for so long as is necessary before handing power back to a civilian government, but cannot always find a civil power that is able to govern. It is faced with the dilemma of serving an oligarchy it knows to be condemned or of itself performing the rôle of party-state for which it is unfitted. Even the younger officers, when impelled to action by political ambitions or by the feeling that they have a rôle to perform, must choose between the alternatives of making the army their party or of breaking the army so that a party may triumph.

As a closed (which does not mean watertight) society, the army cannot allow the formation and triumph of a new class which, after all, would take over the social rôle which only the army could perform or could have performed. The irreconcilable enmity between the military society and the new class probably derives from the identity of the mission which both see themselves as performing. This, at any rate, is what both the Peruvian and the Brazilian situations lead one to believe.

IV

Foreign Pressures

1. *Anti-Imperialism as a Problem and as a Pretext*

Anti-imperialism—most frequently understood as anti-Americanism—is a constant theme in most propaganda tracts and in the programmes and manifestos of political movements in Latin America. It can mobilise the masses. It ensures success to any orator. It can reconcile, for a while, at any rate, divergent factions. Its emotional power is continually utilised by all political movements, from Mexico to Chile.

Like any concept which has mass appeal, this anti-imperialism feeds on, and is composed of, countless different elements, some of which are rational and can be analysed, others of which are psychological and harder to grasp. The extreme sensitivity of public opinion leads the politician, whether he be in power or in opposition, to avoid examining and revealing the exact terms of international relations and to content himself with symbolic generalities. In extreme cases, one finds (as in Uruguay) a verbal anti-Americanism, even though the economy and the working of political institutions are little influenced by the United States; or (as in Mexico) the maintenance of a popular anti-Americanism in a situation where the inter-relationships of their financial systems connect the two countries indissolubly.

At the root of anti-imperialism there probably lies a deep and frustrated nationalism. Very relevant here is the question

as to whether it is expressed in terms of the whole continent—
americanidad—(as it was with Simon Bolívar), claiming spiritual
roots in classical antiquity or using the vocabulary of the French
Revolution to exalt the diverse racial mixtures of the continent
as foreshadowing a new civilisation that, while heir to that of
Europe, will surpass it through the richness of its contradictions;
or whether it is bounded by the narrower compass of nation-
states. Every party and every school of theorists in Latin
America suffers from a tendency to present its doctrine or its
experience as being valid for the whole continent. Time has
passed since the struggles for independence, and the two
dimensions—national and continental—of nationalism are now
clearer.

One can see this first contradiction in the natural suscepti-
bility shown by popular feeling in the case of a country's neighbours. Even today, the mobilisation plan of the Argentine army
is conceived of essentially in relation to Chile, and that of the
Chilean army in relation to Argentina. The problems arising
from regional co-operation remain without solution and become
sometimes the source of festering quarrels, for nationalist
passions affect the behaviour of governments. Hence the question of Bolivia's access to the sea; hence, too, the disputes among
Peru, Ecuador and Brazil regarding the development of the
Amazon region.

As state nationalism gathered strength, the tendency towards
expansion or regional hegemony developed among the stronger
nations. These are natural phenomena and it is in good taste
not to mention them, under the pretext that anti-imperialism
can exist only in relation to the United States, Europe, or the
Soviet Union. Nevertheless, it is Argentine pressure rather than
American intervention that is responsible for the strangling of
the Paraguayan economy.

Anti-imperialism, with its general justification of Latin
American solidarity, is thus juxtaposed with state nationalism.
It is both the result of a series of real factors which derive from

93

a number of common relationships vis-à-vis the United States, and of affective factors deriving from a feeling of national impotence and the fond hope of the possibility of Latin American power. Oppositions, hatreds and jealousies among the individual countries of Latin America do not rule out the idea of a 'trade union' for common defence, even of the hope and will to construct a common destiny.

These points of view cannot be derived from the 'cult of general ideas' alone, but must also be based on the study of the problems to be solved and of the human and material means necessary for their solution. In other words, anti-imperialism can be of benefit only if one disregards the sentimental literature that serves to perpetuate confusion and prevent the carrying out of concrete measures.

A pertinent critique of the inefficacy of the anti-imperialist attitudes of the Latin American left has been put forward by an excellent economist under the pseudonym of 'Espartaco'.[1] He insists on the need to take account of national situations, of the type of industries that exist or are possible in competition with foreign enterprises, and also of the relative importance of the stake that an industry with private capital installed in a foreign country can represent for a nation, be it imperialist or not. No real anti-imperialist policy can be conceived, far less put into practice, without this exact knowledge of individual situations and without an appreciation of the interests at stake which can lead a government like that in Washington, according to whether it believes these interests to be vital or not, to safeguard or sacrifice American property in Latin America.

It would be hard not to agree ['Espartaco' writes], that the 'economic independence' of a country depends, not on political pronouncements or on 'verbal anti-imperialism', but essentially on its degree and type of economic development. More important than manifestos and attitudes are the structure of foreign trade, the degree of differentiation of the internal productive system, the objective possibility of re-acting to foreign threats, or the possession of autonomous centres of decision-taking and implementing. Nevertheless, these main problems have rarely deserved the *concrete*—as distinct from the oratorical—attention of left-wing Marxist groups. . . . All the tactical moves of the Jacobin left as regards property-owners have been decisively dictated by 'external variables', that is, by circumstances related to the international situation, be it the supporting or expression of solidarity with the Soviet Union or, alternatively, the estab-lishment of some kind of anti-imperialist association with various groups of the 'national bourgeoisie'.

The oligarchic castes call themselves, and are, anti-imperialist simply because they are opposed to any form of change and because the introduction of imported capital, techniques and structures, which are beyond their control, is one of the charac-teristics of imperialist penetration. The 'middle classes' are anti-imperialist in conviction in so far as they identify imperialism with the rational functioning of the administration, with the elimination of political or family *clientelae*, or with the disappear-ance of the ideal formula, 'be born with a scholarship, live with a public job, die with a pension' (*nacer becado, vivir empleado, morir jubilado*). The 'available' intellectuals are anti-imperialist for exactly the opposite reasons. It is the valorisation of national resources for foreign benefit or the keeping fallow of these resources by the same foreigners that makes them rebel and demand change under the guidance of a national ruling political class.

Anti-imperialism, the meeting-place of all tendencies—some conservative and opposed to change, others reformist or revolu-tionary—cannot thus be considered a single phenomenon, any more than can 'imperialism' itself. For, if confusion is fostered by the anti-imperialists in order to mobilise all resentments into one movement which each participant thinks will ultimately redound to his benefit and his alone, further confusion is fostered by the many representatives, defenders or beneficiaries of the foreign interests.

There is no lack of theories, changing and contradictory, to justify United States' policies in Latin America. From the first formulation of the Monroe Doctrine in 1823 (which considered as dangerous for the peace and safety of the United States any attempt that the European powers might make to extend their system to any part whatsoever of the hemisphere) to the defence of free enterprise, one could gather a rich crop of theses and formulas. To sort them all out, taking account of the different regions and historical situations, would demand a volume in itself. One can, nevertheless, usefully distinguish certain permanent features of the various policies of the United States.

One must distinguish first between Central America and the Caribbean on the one hand, and the southern part of the continent on the other. In the former, American commercial interests have solid roots, and for some small countries the economic infrastructure was controlled by American countries to the point that the United States considered the region as its 'zone of influence'. In the latter, the most important phenomenon was the penetration of British, French and German influences.

This important difference between the 'direct' and 'indirect' interests of the United States, which corresponded to geographical distance, can be seen throughout the history of the relationship between American and Latin American capital. The decision, taken at the end of April 1965, to disembark troops in the Dominican Republic cannot be explained rationally—even from Washington's point of view—in strategic, economic or political terms. But it corresponds perfectly to the conditioned reflex: the Caribbean forms part of the immediate American periphery.

Furthermore, the goals of the United States, and the means

employed to attain them, cannot be easily defined, for they are determined sometimes by economic interest-groups, sometimes by the State Department, and sometimes, more recently, by the military. Co-ordination occurs only in times of crisis, and for most of the time each carries out an independent policy. No official and responsible body has ever given a long-term definition of the policy of the United States towards Latin America or of the type of relationships which are envisaged. Most frequently, decisions are taken not with regard to the concrete problems that arise between the Latin American countries and Washington but with regard to considerations of 'global strategy'. In the post-war period, for example, President Truman spoke in 1949 of military aid, defence, the strengthening of the United Nations, economic and technical assistance programmes. In 1956, President Eisenhower presented his programme of mutual security—in which he included Latin America—as a system of defence against the Soviet threat. President Kennedy inaugurated a new period of support for social reforms and economic development; but President Johnson returned to a more conservative position and replaced the team of advisers in charge of Latin American affairs.

The lack of defined long-range goals and the tendency to consider the Latin American countries as of only secondary importance in the struggle for world leadership gratuitously strengthen an already virulent anti-Americanism. So much so that North American proposals worthy of consideration meet only with scepticism or out-of-hand rejection as a matter of principle. The support given by the United States to the Bolivian revolutionary régime attracted less attention than the support for the opponents of Castro. Likewise, no goodwill can arise on the part of the advocates of change in Latin America from the United States' support and maintenance of the armed forces of each country, particularly since this aid is budgeted in Washington on the same terms as technical assistance or economic aid.

Similarly, the permanent confusion between the policy of the State Department and the defence of American private interests fosters the equally permanent anti-American campaign. As W. S. Woytinsky remarked after a research visit to Latin America:

> Many representatives of the United States believe that a pro-American attitude should be expressed by means of government abstention in the economic sphere, by reliance on private enterprise, by a welcome given to foreign investment. If, on the other hand, a government decides to reserve for itself the search for oil or to rely on a public regional development plan, it is felt to be guilty of anti-American tendencies and even of being pro-communist.[2]

There is, in fact, a kind of missionary spirit among most us officials who attempt to sell their commercial, industrial and even institutional arrangements. The arrangements produce better results than the disorder, the muddles and the improvisation of the 'tropical' countries, but those who advocate them have little regard for the situations and traditions of Latin America and none at all for the rage which this advice provokes among those who are subjected to it.

The continual to-and-fro between advice, threats, aid, strategic considerations, imperatives of world politics, intervention, moralistic sermons and the calculation of dividends —this, far from fostering the creation of an 'American party', prompts the mobilisation of anti-American crowds even when us actions are not responsible for the catastrophe or the stagnation, and when those who are responsible are to hand.

The desire for order, with which immobility is confused, continually gets in the way of the diplomacy or, let us repeat, of the several diplomacies of Washington. The element of order is usually a strong man or an army: more stable, generally speaking, partners in a dialogue than a series of organisations which struggle in rivalry among themselves. The choice should not be made according to the criterion of apparent stability, which itself generates violence that does not lead to any reform, but according to the criterion of the transformations that are necessary. Most of the 'proponents of order' on the national scale are those who, by exporting their capital to Switzerland, the United States or Mexico at a rate often too fast for American aid to catch up with it, are destroying the conditions of possible social justice.

It goes without saying that, if pro- or anti-imperialist attitudes reflect either a desire to maintain the social status quo or to break with it, in either case the true facts of the case are distorted. The important point is to concentrate on the basic problems so as to specify the exorbitant privileges of certain companies and control the struggle for their suppression. It is a task which has not yet been carried out but which the needs of social renewal will make indispensable. The problem of copper in Chile was never so clearly put as after the massive electoral campaigns of 1964 and 1965. The problem of oil in Peru had never been so freely discussed in public until the coming to power of the young Acción Popular party of President Belaúnde.

A kind of intermittent discussion takes place between the proponents of the *abrazo*, of an embrace between the United States and Latin America, and those who opt for simple and straightforward coexistence. If the relations between North and South America were to be established on the basis of an exact inventory of the interests, benefits and losses of each one, instead of being blown by the breezes of sentimental and humanitarian considerations (which nobody believes in), agreements could probably be reached more easily and more solidly, and their precision would contribute to the exact measurement of the degree and limits of their strategic and economic relationship.

The character of Latin American production—raw materials and foodstuffs—makes these economies fragile and vulnerable, just as the contrast between the Northern colossus and the fragmentation of the Southern family can only lead to feelings of frustration. What one can ask of Washington is that it should not present its civilisation and way of life as being the result of a moral and philosophical attitude but as a simple fact, and that it should define, in as non-literary a way as is possible, what it considers to be in its short-term and long-term interests to offer to the peoples of Latin America. Likewise, one would hope that the mouthpieces of the Latin American countries should state precisely what they intend to impose on the United States or what they expect to obtain from it. Greater precision in the demands that are made would probably contribute to locating the internal social factors that hamper the normal development of a country's economy. This naming of the obstacles to social development would produce the double benefit of making possible not only a concrete anti-imperialist policy but also a real struggle against indigenous privileged groups, even when these wave the banner of national independence.

There are solid reasons which justify the complaints of Latin Americans when they speak of their dependence on foreign capital, but it is less easy to justify their persecution complex. For, while it is true that, out of the $13,600 million of invested capital in 1959, $8,200 million were held by Americans, the export of Latin American capital to safer and more stable countries amounted to $4,000 million.

It is true that the fluctuations of prices in the world market for minerals and agricultural products hamper the drawing up and implementation of a programme of economic transformation and modernisation. Yet the increase in volume and in value of Latin American production of raw materials—mainly oil, copper, lead and zinc—depends on the rapid and continuous growth of the industrialised regions of Europe and North America. Nor should one overlook the fact that, in regard to the production of foodstuffs, such countries as Argentina and Uruguay have been unable to face the competition of new nations and increase their output commensurately with the increase in world demand.

Latin American social structures, the lack of imagination of the privileged castes, and the constant maintenance of unproductive *clientelae* are, together with the mercantilist spirit of the holders of foreign capital and the situation in the world markets, equally responsible for the slow development of the subcontinent's economies. One must admit that these internal structures can be changed, and this is a task for which Latin Americans themselves are responsible.

From several points of view, it appears that the contradictions between the single-product economies of Latin America and the complex industrial economies become interdependencies as soon as one looks at the problem with world economic development in mind. This does not mean that the peoples of Latin America must patiently wait for the international situation to improve and provide them with the possibility of an industrial take-off. On the contrary, what it does mean is that the efforts of the countries of the subcontinent should be directed towards the mobilisation and exploitation of their resources within the framework of a world market whose structure must be taken as given. This mobilisation presupposes the elimination of the dead wood and the brake on development represented by the unproductive privileged classes and the corruption that they have installed or overlooked so as to maintain their own position. This valorisation can only be made on the basis of a sound forecast of the probable role of Latin American resources and production in the world economic scene at present and in the foreseeable future. As the Mexican economist Víctor Urquidi puts it:

It is a pity that, to my knowledge, there does not exist a general study of the historical development of Latin America in, say, the nineteenth century, which establishes a direct link between the growth of Latin American exports and given developments in the different industries in Europe and in the United States or given changes in the structure of consumer demand. . . . What should really occupy the attention of those who study the external aspects of the growth of the Latin American economy is not that it finds itself too dependent on the others—it has always been linked to them—but the possibility that the countries with a higher standard of living and productivity may become self-sufficient and cease to buy Latin American products or buy them at a very slow rate. When the advanced economies no longer need to buy Latin American raw materials and foodstuffs, 'dependence' will have come to an end. But so will the forces that generate development.[3]

2. *Russians and Chinese*

The method of classifying Latin American revolutionary movements according to their pro-Soviet or pro-Chinese sympathies is of undeniable interest for the study of the international repercussions of the Sino-Soviet split. If one goes no further, however, this classification does not assist the understanding of national or regional situations, and runs the risk of becoming a game: sticking little flags on a map of the sub-continent and interpreting their tactical and strategic importance according to the rules of those modern *Cafés du Commerce*, diplomatic circles and editorial offices.

One must first of all evaluate the strength of the Communist movements effectively linked to Moscow and Peking. Over the last forty years, militants, agents and Soviet secret services have struggled hard to create Communist parties and organisations which would assist in the victory of Russian international policy. The net result of this gigantic effort, for which material means were not lacking and which frequently took place in favourable social circumstances, has been meagre. In Mexico, Argentina, Brazil and Venezuela—the key countries—the Communist forces are not imposing. Where social transformations have profoundly altered the old structures, as in Bolivia, the Communist party is a marginal force, capable only of tipping the balance. In Chile, the only Latin American country where the Communist party has a house of its own, an apparatus with roots, and electoral power, its influence has not reached the level where it can hope for power.

Slow transformations and sudden changes take place without the Communist party. The vast popular movements that have characterised periods of crisis or express a deep desire for change slip out of its control: APRA in Peru, the MNR in Bolivia, Peronism in Argentina were born and developed outside it, in spite of it and against it, even when fortuitous circumstances produced tactical alliances or coincidences in their plans of action. The only experience which has recently brought to Soviet diplomacy an important but cumbersome and difficult ally, that of the Cuban Revolution, owed nothing, as far as its sources and moving spirits were concerned, to the International or to the local Communist party.

There have been many reasons for this relative lack of success, but two must be emphasised here. Communist propaganda was aimed principally at the working class, while this class was small and still inchoate, and while its militants had already been influenced by other schools of thought. For years, the main efforts of the party were directed towards the conquest, or destruction, of what already existed, and in any case had no decisive rôle in social change. On the contrary, national political formations took shape with the middle classes as their basis. These offered ample possibilities in the field of social and political demands, and their rise seemed equally profitable for the urban and agricultural labourers. Experience has shown that Haya de la Torre was right and the eminent theorists of the Third International wrong at the time of the great disputes of the 1920s.

Since then, the Communist parties in Latin America have adapted themselves and used more general formulas; but—and here we find the second factor responsible for their slow progress—they have come up against parties that saw themselves, too, as being *unique* and whose apparatuses covered all the social strata from the students to the peasants.

Nowadays one must add a further item to the debit side of the Communist parties' account: they have become rigid bureaucracies. In Buenos Aires, in Rio, in Mexico and in Santiago, Communist leaders have clung to their positions, achieved by political acrobatics, like retired soldiers to their pensions. The so-called 'Khrushchev line' suits them down to the ground and they have experienced no personal difficulty in defending it. To insinuate oneself into the legal political framework, to play one's rôle in it, to be wary of any adventure, and to put anti-Americanism to good use are political formulas that allow one to use a revolutionary vocabulary without running the risks of exposing oneself.

In circumstances of extreme social tension, the old *aparatchikis* are incapable of retaining the youthful enthusiasts who, seduced by its revolutionary literature, come to the party and then leave it, disillusioned by its bureaucratic methods. One witnesses, as a consequence, the mushrooming of tiny and ephemeral dissident organisations which bring together the outsiders of the party, pushed to one side by its leaders, the remnants of old schisms and the young volunteer activists. Sometimes, too, one sees the renaissance or reunification of Socialist parties which have shed their European ideologies and express themselves in terms of ideologies of the moment. Such is the case in Chile and in Uruguay.

Is, then, a 'Chinese International' shepherding together the lost children of the Russian International? For that to happen, the Chinese International would have to exist. Signs of its presence in Latin America are rare. Here and there, of course, one can find offices that collect subscriptions for the magazine *Pekin Informa* or centres which publish Spanish translations of Maurice Thorez's letter to the *Peking Daily*. But for the time being, there is no sign of an active Chinese organisation in the sub-continent.

Certainly, there are innumerable little magazines, groups and 'fronts' which openly declare their pro-Chinese tendency or express their sympathy with it. However, this phenomenon should probably be interpreted as representing, not the effects of Chinese propaganda (except very indirectly), but the need felt by most of the militants to participate in an international movement that gives them greater self-confidence and protects them from discouragement and isolation. They call themselves pro-Chinese so as not to have to face the fact that they are the products of a purely local situation, but they are not members of a new International. Perhaps they hope for one, but as yet it has no reality. Likewise, at the ideological level, many young rebels call themselves 'Trotskyists', not because they have found in Trotsky's writings an answer to their problems, but simply because they feel the need to belong to a school of thought.

The only continental network which has established itself and been active has been that of *Fidelismo*, hastily formed by intellectuals in search of a cause, by traditional fellow-travellers, by Stalinist agents, by some young and well-meaning idealists, and, for more serious matters, by members of G2* who are attached to Havana rather than to Moscow or to Peking. After the first enthusiasm has died down, the corrosive effect of internal struggles, attempts to put them to one side on the part of the Communist parties, the manipulations of impatient politicians and the departure of militants disappointed with the course taken by Castro's régime, have rapidly disbanded the Committees for the Support of the Cuban Revolution. What remains is a kind of humus in which a few rare plants still grow, but which cannot produce any kind of disciplined organisation.

This chaos does not, however, limit revolutionary effervescence; on the contrary, it feeds it. Discontents, which

* Castro's political police force.

frequently lead to opposing claims, find an ideological façade in pseudo-Marxist vocabularies or in the arsenal of Communist plans of action. This chaos reveals the heterogeneity of the opposition movements and of the forces of change, and its general and permanent character reveals the kinship that links them. A group, a movement or a party does not spring from the collectively expressed will of a definite class or any given social stratum. It reflects the desires and hopes of a more or less numerous category of 'availables' within the conglomerate of the 'middle classes'.

This is not a new phenomenon. There has never, except in syndicalist form, existed a workers' party or a peasant party in Latin America. Social tensions and conflicts have long been exploited by organisations arising out of the middle classes and led by intellectuals. What *is* new is that the development of the middle classes, constantly increasing and being renewed, no longer corresponds to the economic possibilities of the present régimes. The army, the civil service, politics, industry and commerce, one after another or simultaneously, have acted as outlets for the contingents who were leaving the colleges and universities. Today the stagnant state of agricultural production and the mediocrity of industry prevent the continued absorption of a proliferating tertiary sector. The traditional outlets can no longer provide jobs, posts or sinecures for the new generation of applicants.

We thus witness a questioning of the whole system on the part of those who cannot hope to benefit from it. The younger generation is the first to launch an attack. At the margin of the traditional parties—right- or left-wing, conservative or radical— forces of opinion begin to take shape. The young are no longer willing to join the traditional ranks or play yesterday's political game, for the stakes are laughable and prospects non-existent. Put more crudely, they are looking for an entirely new way of accumulating capital.

The vocabulary may be extremist; they may frequently launch appeals for social revolution, and invoke the historic mission of the proletariat or the revolutionary potential of the landless peasants; but, nevertheless, the leaders of these groups are not workers or peasants, or even Socialists in the libertarian and egalitarian sense of the term. Their basic organisations are formed as centres of agitation, as springboards for the conquest of power, rather than as elements for social reconstruction. The state is considered to be the only machine able to transform, to plan and to create.

In certain countries—as in Uruguay, where social conflicts are still compatible with the continued functioning of the régime—the extremist students and professionals end up by becoming integrated in a limited society and using proclamations of support for external revolution as their means of evasion. And where an entrepreneurial bourgeoisie creates modern industries and consequently new jobs, a part of this middle class finds a way out and abandons its demands for reform.

The most characteristic example of the extreme mobility and agility of those in the intellectual strata who feel themselves excluded from the benefits of the old social and political system can be found in Frondizi's Argentina in 1958. There was an influx of extremists into the ministerial offices, into the propaganda services and into the countless committees of experts set up to assure businessmen of the good intentions of the régime. The result was the partial depletion of the most left-wing movements; and of the theories held only a short time previously, all that remained was a vaguely progressive vocabulary.

On the other hand, where social pressures correspond to the ripening of deep antagonisms, the new contingents exploit discontents, demand a complete restructuring of society and aim at the centres of power. The success of Acción Popular in Peru can be explained both by the apathy engendered among the masses by the sluggishness with which APRA attempted to seize power and by the stalemate arising out of the clash between the two 'totalitarian' apparatuses, APRA and the army. Immediately there emerged new organisations led by intellectuals, feeding on the Indians' hunger for land and demanding a complete reshaping of the social system.

The technique for seizing power invented in Cuba and systematised in the form of a theory by 'Che' Guevara shortly afterwards, has provided a convenient schema for the 'new wave' of intellectuals. This thesis, which does not attempt to conceal a certain contempt for the revolutionary desires and capacities of either workers or peasants, has contributed, among the more radical intellectuals, to a *prise de conscience* of their new possibilities. Of course, as it stands, the theory is inapplicable to most parts of Latin America. It does, however, provide the essential formula, the schema for the movement which adopts it: namely, the rise of a new political class.

In only one country—Colombia—do the guerillas correspond to a spontaneous movement, with the participation of more or less solid groups of between 10 and 500 men acting in several rural areas and controlling some sectors. They are not the result of foreign initiatives but perpetuate a long tradition of violence between Conservatives and Liberals. The bloodiest period of this violent tradition was that which followed the assassination of the Liberal leader Jorge Elicer Gaitán on April 9, 1948. The crime was followed by an explosion of popular rage in Bogotá and by a wave of massacres throughout the country. Many areas controlled by the Liberals remained in a state of rebellion against the central government, and several 'constitutions' were drawn up regulating the relationship between the civil authorities and the military command. The best known is that of the *llanos*, where the unit for the nomination of representatives to the 'Congress' was the group of families who provisioned themselves with meat at the same place.

The civil war which put most of Colombia in a state of

continual effervescence until the 'national' agreement between the Liberals and the Conservatives—establishing that the presidency would be occupied alternately by each of the two parties—has not entirely died out. It is a case not only of *bandoleros* and the remnants of armed groups, but also of men caught up in the unquenchable hatreds of vendettas and of young men without roots. All of these are factors which favour the existence of a guerilla movement. The authority of the central government is hard to enforce in the contested areas. That it is imposed at all is due to the army, whose methods harass the population as much as do those of the terrorists.

For several years, extreme left-wing organisations have been attempting to influence or to control these guerillas and to profit from the decomposition and inefficacy of the two main traditional parties. It does not appear, however—and this opinion is supported by that of careful Colombian observers— that the articulation between the tiny extremist groups of the urban centres, jealous rivals one of another, and the natural formations of the peasant areas, generally attached to a local leader, can become established and lead to a large-scale revolutionary movement.[4]

One could carry the analysis further, almost to the point of caricature, and say that among the bomb-throwing son or daughter of a doctor or banker in Caracas, the young technocrat of the inter-American economic organisations, the 'Nasserist' army captain, the Christian Democrat militant and the activist in a revolutionary organisation, there are no class differences, only (given different contexts and situations) variations of degree in the evaluation of their possibilities of integration into existing or changing societies.

As for the Russian and Chinese seductions, they appear on an important but limited level. The exploitation of rivalries between the world blocs is a perspective that is common to all the new régimes who are both eager for loans, credit and technical aid, and anxious to lay hands on their own national resources.

This is not a trend that is peculiar to Latin America. Nor should one forget that, in 1959, only 5 per cent of Latin American exports went to the Soviet Union, whereas Europe and the United States received 30 per cent and 50 per cent respectively.

V

Situations and Experiences

1. Between Words and Reality

Between the written law and the real functioning of social mechanisms there is a great distance. In most situations, the world of official texts and that of the relationships between citizens contradict each other. Constitutional principles, the judiciary, the police, social legislation, the press—these are only some of the fields where abundant examples could be found of the difference between the society that exists on paper and the society that exists on the ground.

Even if in certain countries there is a respect for the law in one field or another of public life—as in Chile, with regard to elections, or in Brazil, with regard to freedom of worship—actual experience is likely to be more accurate than official texts and declarations. Unless one fully understands this, one would have to accept General Stroessner's professions of democratic faith, to admire the virtues of *habeas corpus* in Mexico, and admit that Bolivian journalists express their thoughts freely. Moreover, such statements are presented only at public ceremonies or in international conferences. No man in the street takes them seriously. The only specialists in these texts are precisely those whose occupation it is to manipulate the law or to stick to the letter rather than the spirit. For ordinary mortals, the Argentine saying remains true: 'It is always the commissary's horse which wins' (*siempre gana el caballo del comisario*).

The lack of correspondence between the law and its application cannot be explained solely by the intervention of illegal but powerful forces, or by a total disregard for regulations on the part of those charged with implementing them. Thus, when in Chile a husband kills his unfaithful wife and receives only two years' imprisonment with stay of execution, whereas a cattle thief will usually be shot without there being, even if he is killed, any judicial proceedings, one is merely witnessing two cases in which the law in Chile yields before two traditions whose validity is accepted by all: that of the *macho* on the one hand,* that of the inviolability of property on the other. In Peru, in Ecuador and in Colombia, the situation is a different one. There, the police and the machinery of justice are prodded into action only when the crime has been committed against a member of the élite. If the victim belongs to an inferior social stratum or does not have the benefit of political protection, they are seized by a kind of paralysis.

Equality before the law presupposes a single society. In Latin America, however, one is frequently faced with several societies, only one of which corresponds to the law. In Chile, for example, the law excluded children under sixteen from entry into cinemas showing films where kisses were long. At home these same children and their younger brothers lived in such promiscuity that it was difficult for them to say who was their father, and could frequently observe their sisters calmly soliciting from the door of the house. Brazilian law condemns racial segregation, but this in no way affects what any observer can easily see for himself: the fact that, as one climbs up the social ladder, the colour of people's skins becomes progressively lighter. Certainly, the 'model' of race relations which operates in Brazil does not correspond to that which the

---

* *Macho*: male. *Machismo* is perhaps best defined as assertive, even swaggering, masculinity.

European has in mind and in terms of which he reacts. The absence of racialism in the terms which a left-wing intellectual is likely to recognise leads him to believe that it does not exist. Even the industrial society of São Paulo cannot hide it, however. Florestan Fernandes, who has spent several years studying the racial problem in São Paulo, has shown that one can still find there today traditional racial attitudes. 'They continue to be strong and active thanks to the concentration in the hands of a single race of income, of social prestige and of power. The situation is more characteristic of a caste society than of a class society'.[1]

The Indian race in Mexico is equal before the law, exalted in official speeches and receives all the benefits of presidentialist democracy. Nevertheless, it still constitutes the greater part of the marginal populations of the illiterate and of the under-nourished. The Indians form an internal colony of several millions. They have no participation whatsoever in public life, and constitute a reserve of labour-power which slowly feeds the peripheries of the large cities, where assimilation finally takes place through hunger and misery. The same holds for most of the countries where there are Indian, *mestizo*, Negro, or mulatto populations. No legal text reflects or justifies the disdainful behaviour of the white (or nearly white) 'élites' towards anything coloured, or the functioning of society by strata.

To remind conscientious revolutionaries, or the faithful signatories of anti-imperialist manifestos, of these situations—which are there for all to see—would not be kind; for the terminology they use to attack the mechanisms of colonialism and neo-colonialism could equally well be applied in San Cristóbal or Mitla.

The constitutional guarantees which protect the press, frequently put forward by governmental spokesmen as an example of the correct functioning of the Latin American democracies, is another case of a hypocrisy so widespread that it ends up by not being noticed at all. It is true that, except for exceptional periods when constitutional guarantees are suspended—military coups, states of siege—the freedom of the press is a firmly anchored tradition in Latin America. Any attempt to prevent its operation, even when a régime based on force comes to power, provokes complaints and protests. Censorship is detested—so much so that even dictatorships, once they feel that their power is firmly established, are inclined to allow the publication of an opposition newspaper: a *coquetterie* which accords well with Latin American folklore and gives them a clear conscience in the face of international opinion.

But the rights enjoyed by newspaper proprietors unfortunately protect neither journalists nor their readers. What editors may publish is determined by a censorship imposed not by the government but by the proprietors. Their position has been described by a journalist as follows:

> The labour market for a journalist is a limited one. There are more would-be journalists, whose numbers are increasing as a result of the schools of journalism, than jobs on the dailies. As a result the journalist . . . finds himself tied to his post and is for this reason forced to exercise self-censorship, self-limitation, and to avoid, by all means possible, antagonising the directors of the newspaper or periodical for which he works. He must take care that his account of events does not weaken or contradict the editorial policy of the newspaper.[2]

In many of the large capitals—Santiago and Bogotá, for example—the main newspaper is owned by a traditional family or by an oligarchic interest-group, who use the newspaper not only to present facts but also to put forward an interpretation of them. The qualities of the editor, the abundance of cultural pages and love for the commercial freedom of the press do not alter the situation.

One should perhaps add that the lot of the reader is not much better in those countries where the daily press is free from the clutches of the oligarchy and its liberalism *pro domo*. One greets with a mixture of amusement and surprise the sight, in the extreme left-wing and anti-government press in Mexico, of the complete texts of the president's long speeches. This publicity given to the opponent is not a sign of objectivity. It can be explained by the fact that a ministerial department distributes newsprint.

The vocabulary used to describe, on paper, the administration, to draw up laws and decrees, to explain the theoretical functioning of institutions, could well be replaced by one more in accord with real nature of these institutions and of those who occupy posts in them. The popular vocabulary is frequently more illuminating. The representative of the workers in Brazilian state institutions is called by the workers themselves a *pelego*: the sheepskin blanket used to cover a horse's back. The image is a clear one. And from the readiness with which a Chilean *peon* calls anybody who wears a tie *jefe* or *patroncito*, one can derive a much more concrete picture of class relations than from reading the official newspaper or listening to parliamentary speeches.

The words or formulas on which official language feeds, and most of the figures in volumes of official statistics, bear little correspondence to real facts and practices. There does not, to my knowledge, exist any study of the commercial activities of members of the armed forces in Peru or in Argentina or in Paraguay or in the countries of Central America. Yet any citizen of these countries could provide vivid details of these activities. The secret is kept only in the texts, and one cannot get to know Latin America from documents. Documents would lead one to believe that the University of Montevideo trains technicians and professionals, a labour-force of use in industrialisation, whereas in fact most of the students are girls studying domestic science and in search of a husband.

In view of this, before presenting the hypotheses which conclude this essay—the definition of the key problems, classes, social forces and power struggles—it will be useful to examine some individual cases, a small sample of the rich variety of phenomena and movements that can be found in Latin America. These will not be exhaustive descriptions or even overall pictures of individual countries: merely notes on particular situations and mechanisms that are significant. These sketches may help the reader to become aware of the variety of the processes that are taking place, and convince him that fashionable theories and simplistic moralising are of no use in understanding them. Even words—labour union, army, self-determination or democracy—take on different meanings in different situations.

2. *Uruguay: the Paradise that Failed*

Before José Batlle y Ordoñez, the government of Uruguay was in the hands of *caudillos*, of the military, or of professional groups (mainly lawyers), and politics was limited to exploiting the advantages offered by power. The economic interests—cattle-rearers, exporters and foreign companies—did not attempt to govern. All they wanted, and got, was the complicity and the favours of the government in power.

As from the last quarter of the nineteenth century and during the first few decades of the twentieth, Batlle concentrated his efforts on political institutions, on the structure of industry, on the economic rôle of the state and on social legislation. By the time of his death in 1929, the country had been transformed, or had, at any rate, taken on entirely new features. For Uruguayans and for international opinion, one of the first 'welfare states' had been born.

One can thus speak of a *Batllista* Uruguay, for it was the will, the ideas and the struggles of one man which shaped the nation. Batlle had little of the ideological sectarian about him. Although he had been influenced by the writings of Rousseau and Comte, and had travelled around Europe in search of constitutional formulas and social programmes, he chose his own ways and means, and the rhythm of change, in terms of the material and human realities of the country. He was the last of the *caudillos* in Uruguay in the sense that his personal influence, his qualities as a man, his aggressiveness and his tenacity were as important as the movement and the institutions he created. He wanted to bequeath them to his country in order to spare it the chaotic and bloody struggles of *caudillismo*. Batlle's massive silhouette evokes paternal wisdom, goodness and responsibility. Consciously or not, his behaviour conformed to the paternal model. His speeches were reasoned and logical, and in contrast with the sonorous rhetoric of popular tribunes. But he did not yield in the face of his adversaries (in 1904, he crushed by force of arms an attempted coup d'état organised by the Blancos), nor was he carried away by his supporters. At the time of the general strike of 1911, addressing the demonstrators from the presidential balcony, he told them that if he were not president he would join them, but warned them against violence and once again proclaimed martial law.

It is not easy to summarise Batlle's thought for it is not a doctrine but a series of convictions and a method of action, held together by his personality rather than by theoretical articulation. Simple ideas which today are commonplace, but which at the time were explosive—individual liberties, national sovereignty, respect for the rules of democracy—were tinged with an original conception of society. In a speech delivered at the congress of the Colorado party in 1925, Batlle defined a near-Socialist philosophy which, while not excluding class conflict, did not consider it essential. 'In fact, property should belong to no one, or rather should belong to all, and the entity that represents everybody should be society. Property, then, should belong to society.' To make his ideas known and to ensure their triumph, Batlle founded a newspaper, *El Día*, which was to become an instrument for ceaseless political education. Around it there gathered the opinion of an urban population dissatisfied with governmental chaos, the emptiness of declarations of formal rights and the predominance of the aristocratic landed classes. Immigration brought him a continuously increasing number of recruits in the form of Europeans already influenced by liberal or revolutionary ideas.

Batlle considered that the normal and stable functioning of democratic institutions could be conceived without the existence of true parties: of organisations, that is, which lead a life of their own, not of committees or groups dependent on a privileged fraction or on the government. The new party envisaged by him would have a social programme, an economic policy and a national frame of reference in order to be able, if the suffrage were favourable to it, to shape the country according to the desires of the majority. The party had to be the means whereby the people participated in government. This was to be achieved by making it the storehouse of the wishes and desires expressed by the citizens, and by permitting the rank and file to control the government of the elected, who were members of the same organisation. It was thus on the basis of 'clubs', connected by zone and by departments, articulated by a national commission and gathered together in a congress, that the Colorado party, under Batlle's direction, became progressively modernised.

At the end of his life, he could be proud of what he had achieved. Individual and public freedoms were ensured. Elections took place normally, without coercion or violence. Proportional representation safeguarded the rights of minorities. The army performed no rôle apart from that assigned to it by the constitution. And, although Batlle's idea of suppressing the presidential office and replacing it with an executive power, a governmental *junta*, was not accepted during his lifetime, the country rallied round the formula a few years after his death, and following the unfortunate experience of Terra's dictatorship. Two main organisations shared public support, one in power and active, the other in opposition, controlling and defending the population against any encroachment by the state. Each department had an autonomous administration.

The achievements of social legislation were considerable. Social security, old-age pensions, a minimum wage and unemployment benefit had been set up by law. Education received an important share of the budget. The university was developing without hindrance. The rights of women, including that of divorce, were guaranteed and respected. Economic problems had been tackled boldly. The state became the manager of public works and organised national enterprises to compete with the foreign enterprises before taking over the latter by compulsory purchase. Mortgage and insurance companies were operating. In the hands of the state were electric power, the administration of the port of Montevideo and a meat refrigeration plant. Subsequently, other autonomous state enterprises emerged to manage basic industries such as cement, alcohol, oil refineries and fishing. Surrounded by disorder and confusion, Uruguay was setting an example. And the pampered inhabitant of this happy country could, and did, say: 'There's no place like Uruguay' (*como Uruguay no hay*).

Today, however, a good many Uruguayans would speak less complacently. 'There are countries where one debates whether the present generation should be sacrificed so as to ensure the welfare of future generations. In Uruguay, the present generation is sacrificed so as to ensure a happy old age for the preceding generation.' This light-hearted but damning definition of Uruguayan democracy was recently put forward by the sociologist Aldo Solari.[3] He is mainly concerned with the burden imposed on the economy by the pension system, but his formula is illuminating with respect to several aspects of social life. Retirement schemes are for the most part near bankruptcy, and payments are subject to considerable delays. They are crushed by the weight of their bureaucracies and not even inflation can remedy their finances. They continue to be run in the *Batllista* spirit: in other words, according to a belief in continual progress achieved with the help of a paternalistic state, while the ministries are year by year dissociating themselves more and more from their deficits.

When the law on old-age pensions was passed in February 1919, it was envisaged that the state should pay an annuity to every person over sixty years of age and to every person, regardless of age, who was considered completely unemployable and who had no other means. Since then, however, and always with the support, the protection or the agreement of the state, many pension schemes were created, each providing supplementary benefits for its members: public servants, workers in state industries, commercial employees and, more generally, all social and professional categories. Other generous laws protect the individual against unemployment and illness, assure him social security and education, are equally impregnated with Batlle's ideological outlook, and contribute to the creation of a communitarian society.

In spite of certain excesses that can be noted in the drawing up of security schemes, and which can partly be explained by the need to bid for votes, these social security provisions seem to have been able to function normally and to develop in a balanced way thanks to the economic expansion of the country, to its seemingly inexhaustible supply of cattle products, and to industrial development. The two World Wars gave pacifist Uruguay a considerable supply of foreign exchange and enabled the *Batllista* programme to be carried out in the economic sphere. Eventually, however, the situation was reversed, despite the impetus provided by the Korean War. Peace is unfavourable to neutral countries. Today, deprived of external stimulants, Uruguay finds that it is not as healthy as it seemed.

The reason is, to take up once again the example of old-age pensions, that Uruguay is an 'old' country. Its median age is one of the highest in Latin America. Immigration no longer disguises the fact except to a minimal degree. Graver still is the fact that Uruguayans are emigrating, and here we touch on a more disquieting general problem. Pensions were comfortable at the time when their level was established, but their value in devalued currency no longer allows their recipients a decent standard of living. Pensions are progressively becoming no more than contributions to income, contributions which must be supplemented by earnings derived from a part-time job or by representing commercial firms. The distinction between earners and pensioners becomes more hazy, and this trend is accentuated by the fact that many earners have several different jobs.

Although based on a clearly enunciated principle—the right of each citizen to an old age free from material worries—the system gives rise to a series of shocking situations. Several handsome pensions are accumulated by high-ranking civil servants and dignitaries while the elderly worker finds it hard, after months or years of applications, to receive his meagre pension, and even then only if he can enlist the support of a political faction or have recourse to an intermediary (for a commission fee) who is more experienced in dealing with a labyrinthine and underpaid bureaucracy which is, for this very reason, all the more susceptible to certain kinds of persuasion. Meanwhile, there are heiresses, married and earning, who continue to receive their deceased fathers' pensions which a particular dispensation has made transferable.

At a meeting of representatives of departmental assemblies in 1900, extraordinary cases came to light, such as that of a pension scheme which, despite a deficit of several million pesos, still continued to lend capital to those of its members who wanted to invest in construction. Nor is this simply an unfortunate excrescence or a regrettable but insignificant exception. Figures for 1963 revealed that 290,000 individuals, out of a population of under 3 millions, were receiving pensions. At the same time, disorder and bureaucratisation extend to the departments of the social services that correspond to active life.

In the administration and the public industries, the number of personnel employed is enormous but the quality of services and the volume of production seem to be inversely proportional to the number of employees. An extreme example is provided by SOYP: an organisation designed to promote the fishing industry. Its main function—and this in a country with an Atlantic coastline—consists in importing tinned fish. The recruitment and maintenance of personnel operates according to family, friendship or political networks far more than according to the criteria of the public interest, productivity and efficiency. Employment in the public services becomes a means of distributing state funds, or, put another way, a means of disguising unemployment. There are, in effect, 200,000 public servants, excluding education, the police and the army. Even taking into account the fact that some of them are productive, this is still an astronomical figure, given the total population of the country.

In many fields, the organisational superstructure corresponds to highly developed societies with expanding economies. The banking system is a good example of this. There are 62 banks in Montevideo and 500 branches spread throughout the interior. The number of employees is comparable with that of a large bank in the United States. The latter, however, will have funds twenty times greater than those of all the Uruguayan banks put together. One can thus legitimately draw the conclusion that this proliferation of aids to industry and commerce constitutes, in the last analysis, a brake on development, and that in the absence of economic prosperity—which would be aided by the banks and which would help them in turn—the main reason for their existence is speculation in all its forms.

Taking the economy as a whole (and statistics do no more than confirm what even the most casual observation leads one to suppose), non-productive activities are more numerous than productive ones. Roughly 45 per cent of the active population belongs to what is usually termed the tertiary sector. But whereas—as in the highly productive economies—the tertiary sector expanded as a result of the modernisation of agriculture and the development of industry, this non-productive population must now be maintained by a sickly industrial sector and an agricultural sector undergoing crisis. There are 250,000 commercial employees: more than the total industrial labour force.

Uruguay exists by virtue of its cattle. The Spanish explorers and conquerors considered the 'oriental' territory of La Plata as a land without resources and of no interest—*tierra de ningún provecho*. It was only after the prodigious multiplication of the first herds disembarked and let loose by Hernandarias at the beginning of the seventeenth century that the abundance of the cattle attracted the cowboys and traders of the provinces beyond the Uruguayan river, whose centre of activities was Santa Fé. This was the period of the *Vaquería del Mar*, in which the beasts were slaughtered, their hides removed, and the carcasses left to be devoured by dogs. Only the hides had any commercial value. It was not until much later, thanks initially to salting techniques and subsequently to refrigeration, that meat became an export product. The land and what fed off it no longer belonged to those who rode over it on horseback and herded the cattle. It had become property. Montevideo, a port held and closed by the Spanish, became after independence the centre for exports. But wealth came from the herds. At the time of the foundation of Montevideo in 1726, there were an estimated 25 million head of cattle. By the end of the last century these cattle resources were regarded as the basis of the economy. The most progressive of the Uruguayan innovators seem to have believed that these resources were, if not inexhaustible, at any rate permanent, and that they would provide a solid foundation for bold projects. However, if modern economists are to be believed, exports of frozen and tinned meat are declining at such a rate that, by 1970, if energetic measures are not taken, Uruguay's share of the world market will have fallen to nothing.

This decline in exports can be explained by a number of factors which have been operative for about the last quarter of a century. Firstly, production—both cattle-rearing and agriculture—is increasing at the feeble annual rate of approximately 1·6 per cent, whereas the rate of population growth is the same and consumption is increasing. Exports are consequently declining. This trend is reinforced by certain changes in the structure of production. Agriculture has expanded at the expense of cattle-rearing. Thus, whereas in 1935 cattle-rearing provided 40 per cent of production from the land, in 1960 this figure had fallen to 30 per cent. Virgin territory has become scarce and the country has virtually exhausted its possibilities of agricultural expansion.

Admittedly, wool exports are being maintained and still provide a considerable supply of foreign exchange, but this alone is not sufficient to support economic development. The case of wool sheds light on the only way of overcoming the cattle-rearing crisis. What is called for is a series of technical improvements aimed at raising productivity per acre. Sheep-farmers have, on the whole, adopted this policy, whereas the *estancieros* who specialise in meat production have not attempted to modernise. This has led the country into stagnation and to a large extent has contributed to the loss of international outlets. Natural prairies which receive no fertiliser and are unprotected against erosion represent approximately 90 per cent of the area given over to cattle-rearing. The problem thus becomes a social one, and the reforms that are necessary, even from a strictly technical point of view, will strike at the traditional class of cattle-rearing landowners who control immense territories of 15,000, 25,000 acres and more.

No solution, other than the restructuring and modernisation of the production of cattle and a few other products (vegetable oils and rice, for example), can at present be envisaged. Industrialisation, even given the stimulus of the First World War, could begin only because exports of agricultural and cattle products were increasing more rapidly than the population and domestic consumption. The main phase of industrial development followed on the world crisis of 1929. Restrictions on the importation of finished goods and support for imports of primary products, combined with a foreign exchange policy favourable to exports, then directed investment towards the creation of new industries and the extension of old ones so as to answer the demand of the national market in terms of consumer goods.

Urban consumption—and principally that of Montevideo, which contains over a third of the population—increases, but the stagnation of the cattle-rearing sector reduces the volume of exports and plays havoc with the balance of trade. Industrial expansion slows down and then stops through the lack of foreign exchange, the limitation of the national market (which is further accentuated by the feeble absorptive capacity of a stagnant rural society), and the increasing burden of state expenditure. In the present situation, the most modern enterprises are faced with excess capacity relative to domestic demand. They cannot, however, invade foreign markets since their prices are not competitive. The entire economic circuit is thus braked or paralysed. Tariff protection has enabled individual firms to secure a monopoly position for certain types of products, since competition does not operate as a stimulant or regulator. Underemployment and open unemployment can no longer be absorbed by the public services or by the tertiary sectors. The main avenues of Montevideo are full of street vendors, some selling smuggled goods or imitations of smuggled goods: an evident sign of unemployed manpower.

One of the main elements in *Batllista* ideology is the search for social harmony by means of the establishment of institutions and the passing of legislation which relieves the citizen, and more particularly the wage-earner, from anxiety or promises him his desires. This systematic elimination of tensions leads, however, to a dangerous apathy and to a widespread belief that initiative and effort are superfluous because the state, the collectivity or the party are the sole purveyors of security and welfare.

Even today, despite the deterioration of the economic situation, social tensions are not acute and strikes, for the most part, take on the character of demands on the public purse. The régime itself is not questioned, nor is the structure of organisation and of the public services. The main conflicts—in urban transport, banks, electricity, telephones—have thus been resolved by the consumer. The cost of transport to the consumer has doubled and that of electricity increased by 96 per cent. The bank employees went on strike in 1963 without proposing to reform the banking system. Their trade union was content with pointing out that the official and unofficial gains of their employers were large enough to permit a proportion of them to be transferred to the employees.

This client mentality obviously contributes little towards the definition of a policy for trade-union action. It explains the fragmentation of the trade-union movement into countless autonomous organisations and the feebleness of the union confederations, which are continually being formed and reformed and are unable to overcome corporativistic barriers or to avoid the squabbles introduced into their ranks by political factions.

Every four years in Uruguay there occurs an election season of several months. Party propaganda is freely made. Among the more direct methods employed by the competitors and their organisations to make their views known are open-air meetings, parades in the central avenues, radio broadcasts, massive poster-plastering, slogans painted on walls and pavements, and banners across the streets and hanging from the trees. Thousands of clubs open their doors and entertain militants, sympathisers and the merely curious. There is popular, not to say massive, participation in the campaign. In contrast with what happens in

Argentina, the urban masses, and more particularly those of the capital and provincial centres, do intervene.

But this explosion of popular democracy should not deceive us. Most of the voters who throng to the clubs make up a *clientela*, not a party. Most of the sympathisers are Blancos or Colorados by family tradition, and consequently faithful. But they think of their party as a potential source of benefits, not as an organisation which will carry out a programme. As for the party programmes, they are largely forgotten or put forward with calculated imprecision. It is as an individual, and not as a member of a class or social grouping, that the elector or club-member expects to be repaid for his support. The distribution of public employment remains the privilege of the two traditional political groupings. Dealings with the administration are easier when both applicant and civil servant are members of the same party, and this expectation provides a further bond of solidarity.

Within the two main movements there exist rival and even antagonistic factions, but their solidarity is ensured by the famous law of the *lemas*. This law authorises all candidacies; for the distribution of the highest offices, however, only those affiliated to one or the other of the two blocs—Blanco or Colorado—are taken into account. It is thus the men of the political machine, the professional politicians, the elected and the candidates, who guide and control the clubs, and not vice-versa. Beneath their open rivalry, there exists between the two groups a solidarity in favour of maintaining the system. This solidarity is further emphasised by the application of the 'Three-Two Rule', which determines the proportion in which public offices will be distributed among the two parties. Another rule establishes that the national junta will be made up of six members of the majority and three of the minority.

The traditional parties—Colorado, now in opposition after nearly a century in power, and Blanco, which took power in 1958—are daily denounced as being responsible for the present mess. At the same time, they are exhorted to take draconian measures to put an end to the crisis. Discontent and opposition are expressed within the system.

The elections in November 1962 allowed two new groupings to try their luck. The Communist party, plus a few nationalist groups, put forward a left-wing Liberation Front. This bizarre title is explained by its magic initials, FIDEL. The Socialist party, which had been taken over by left-wing intellectuals and swollen by a few Blanco dissidents, entered the contest under the name of Unión Popular. The two experiments were equally unsuccessful. In attempting to play the same game as the two giants, the small left-wing parties were clearly at a disadvantage. They had nothing to offer: no jobs, no letters of introduction. They received votes mainly from intellectuals, academics and petty bourgeois: in other words, from those who already had direct contacts with the administration and who could thus do without political intermediaries.

The extreme left is an intellectual movement, and this is significant. The signatures at the foot of the manifesto which launched Unión Popular were for the most part those of professors, lawyers, writers and doctors. The announcement of the Communist party's candidates is traditionally made twice: one is for the 'masses', the other is for the intellectuals. Why did the two fronts not unite? The 'theories', the 'analyses' and the pseudo-revolutionary literature with which the left is flooded do not help to explain the problem. The main reason has little theoretical basis. The Uruguayan Communist party, like most of its Latin American counterparts, is directed by a group of veteran and unshakable *aparatchikis*. No young man can hope to enter an organisation whose leaders consider themselves the sole repositories of changing truths. Nor, on the other hand, is there any hope in the foreseeable future of the party's taking power. The young and not-so-young rebels, and all those who find the traditional mechanisms of promotion outdated, emigrate to the parties, groups and sects of the extreme left which cluster at the fringes of the Communist party.

Their doctrine is a confused and fluid amalgam of nationalism, not entirely free from a nostalgia for the *gaucho* tradition; of anti-imperialism, all the more violent for not having a concrete object; of support for rapid industrialisation ('there can be no independence without heavy industry'); and of imported intellectual fashions: first Sartre, then Castro, now Mao Tse-tung.

The desperate need for a popular movement which would demand structural reforms and shatter the torpor of a bankrupt welfare state will be answered neither by narrow corporativist labour unions who have forgotten their collective rôle nor by the verbal delirium of intellectuals excited by what goes on abroad but indifferent to national problems. Nor is it likely that the business or the landowning communities will reveal themselves possessed of the spirit of adventure.

The country seems thus to be threatened by two dangers. One is born of the need for order and could lead to reaction and authoritarianism. The other would arise from the replacement of the philanthropic state by an Alliance for Progress which handed out gifts and credits without demanding prior reforms. The only way out would seem to be the possibility that the small nuclei of technicians who make up for their lack of numbers by enterprise and energy and who have been trained in economic forecasting and planning might take over and begin a new chapter in Uruguayan history.

3. *Argentina: The Trade-Union Morass*

Twelve years of Peronism (1943-55), the last of which were dictatorial, proved insufficient to tame the Argentine labour movement: Socialists, libertarians and syndicalists controlled the key unions. The Justicialista landslide, government pressures, the complicity of the forces of order and the vast orchestration of official propaganda could not prevent stubborn resistance to the Peronist attempt at taking over the trade unions. In the meat-processing plants, which were later considered Justicialista strongholds, there were violent struggles between Peronists and Anarchists. At the general assembly which, in 1943, decided which was to be the fate of the organisation, members of both sides were armed. When Peronist pistols were brandished, others were drawn on the opposing side. Both gave way, but a chair-and-bottle fight ensued. The general committee, composed of thirteen members, had to decide, and the Peronists won by seven votes to six. The development of the Peronist unions was marked by rebellions and by attempts by individuals and groups to assert their independence. But the structuring of the régime, the even more monolithic character of the system and the decisive influence of the power of the state rendered these deviations more and more difficult; soon there remained, for the transmission of official orders, nothing but a hierarchy made up of clients of the régime. There were no longer any legitimate representatives of the trade unions themselves.

The expansion of industry, which until then had not been firmly established and was still largely artisan in character, made the setting up of a new union apparatus easier. Many organisations were established at the initiative of the régime. The old union structure, organised according to craft or trade, no longer corresponded to the patterning of new and expanding industries. After the end of the Second World War, the new orientation of Soviet diplomacy led the Communists to abandon their former strongholds to the Peronist apparatus. The sole positive achievement of Stalinist influence on Argentine union organisation—the transformation of countless builders' trade unions into a massive industry-based organisation—only assisted the centralising tendency of Peronist integration. Resistance to corporativist *justicialismo* was maintained only in a few 'historically outmoded' but still active trades, like the tile-workers.

In the sectors that were already organised, the Peronist advance encountered obstacles that could only be removed by state intervention. The commercial employees, the railway workers and the shipworkers could not be persuaded, crushed or intimidated. Their organisations had finally to be taken over by state-designated 'commandos'. Strikes—such as that of the shipworkers in 1953, which lasted more than three months—opposed fractions of the 'true' working class and the policy of control implemented by the régime. Individual reactions on the part of sectors that had been entirely 'Peronised' provoked further conflicts. One such was the violently crushed steelworkers' strike of 1953. One of its organisers, Augusto Vandor, is now once again secretary of the Steelworkers' Union, and still a 'Peronist'.

Thus, when the combined intervention of the army, the navy and the air force put an end to the Peronist régime in September 1955, a solid but fragmented force was available for the task of rebuilding a trade-union movement. Without much difficulty, large federations—such as Fraternidad, which embraced the railwaymen, the federation of typographical workers, the federation of commercial employees, and the bank employees' federation—resumed their activities, frequently under the same leadership that had been violently removed by the Peronists. But the spontaneous recovery of the traditionally democratic unions only partially solved the problem of workers' organisation. The industrial sector remained under Peronist control. The union administration installed under Perón remained active and controlled considerable resources and a large number of clients.

Two blocs soon formed, the 'Sixty-Two' and the 'Thirty-Two'. The latter embraced the truly representative organisations in which membership was nearly always voluntary. Out of a total union membership of $2\frac{1}{2}$ million, the theoretical total of organised employees, it controlled more than a million. They lacked aggressive spirit, either because they were too concerned with the 'purification' measures that had to be carried through by the 'Revolución Libertadora' in order to break Peronism or because they came up against the manoeuvring of successive governments, which spared and even favoured the Peronist groups in order to neutralise or conciliate them. In their efforts to defend the working class, the groups of the Thirty-Two did not obtain any concessions from management. Their demands for wage increases and pension readjustments were rejected, and they were thus handicapped in their attempts to win over working-class opinion.

In 1957, at the reunification congress of the Central Union Federation (CGT), the 'Thirty-Two' were already discouraged and did not put up the struggle which would have broken the Peronist façade. The 'Sixty-Two' claimed to represent a slightly larger number of unions than did the 'Thirty-Two'. This paper majority gave them grounds for claiming a majority in the federation's administrative organisation and for giving a political slant to the CGT. But these figures, which for many were suspect, had not been checked; moreover, the main issue was whether or not the representativeness of union leaderships set up under an authoritarian régime and speaking in the name of passive unions (dues were automatically deducted from wages) should be recognised. More than a question of statistics, it was the entire concept of a union movement that was at issue. Only a small and militant minority was willing to focus the debate round this issue, and the congress ended in uproar. It was only in 1961, six years after the downfall of the Peronist régime, that a kind of modus vivendi was established between the two factions, on the basis of equal shares in the provisional running of an ill-defined CGT. The 'declaration' of the provisional commission included a series of ambiguous formulas in which each side could find a justification for its own methods and aims.

What was more important was the fact that the Peronist camp was no longer threatened by a massive assault. Encouraged by the electoral successes enjoyed by its 'political' programme and by the fact that its conception of vertical obligatory unionism—whose advantages for trade-union officials are clear—was no longer rejected by all the independent leaders, it took the initiative once again. The frontiers of union geography seemed for the time being to have been fixed, at least as regards the larger organisations. Opposition groups could no longer plan or even hope to obtain a majority. In the Peronist unions, the firmly controlled organisation did not allow any propaganda on behalf of divergent opinions, and in the independent unions the experience of the militants was sufficient to contain the assault of the Peronist-Communist coalition.

Whether discussions took place behind closed doors or publicly in the democratic Socialist groups, it became clear that a not insignificant body of militants within the independent sector admitted that military intervention would represent a solid guarantee against the return of the Peronist adventurers. The support of these militant anti-Peronists in the trade-union movement was an important element in the success of the military coup in 1955 which drove Perón from power. This acceptance of the lesser of two evils clearly could not be supported on doctrinal grounds. It was purely tactical and provided neither a framework for restructuring the union movement nor a plan of action. Given a situation which emphasised the feebleness of the independent workers' movement, opinions as to the future and how to reinforce the democratic sector varied enormously.

In fact, for several months after the coup, a group of union leaders struggled to persuade the military to content themselves with holding back the Peronist commandos and to leave the field free for the independents to reorganise the CGT. One of the most brilliant and decisive of these men was Juan Corral, leader of the railwaymen, who undertook, without concealing his unionist and anti-militarist convictions, to inform the *gorila* circles of the need for them to act as guarantors of public freedom while leaving to the unions the task of reorganising democratic life. Corral's influence—he died in 1961—does not seem to have been negligible. He helped some of the military to realise the extent of the adventure they had begun and the gravity of the social problems which they tended to want to solve by decree. At any rate, men like General Menéndez expressed some surprise at discovering that there were leaders of a proletarian movement who were neither corrupt nor corruptible and who spoke the same language whether they were in prison or surrounded by the wood panelling of an officers' mess.

If Corral's position reflected a desire to rescue the trade-union movement, the recourse to military protection corresponded, for a number of other militants, to a deep scepticism as regards the possibilities of reforming the union movement from within. Some union bureaucrats hoped, and still hope, that union headquarters would be opened to them by bayonets and that the command of the CGT would be offered them by the Ministry of War.

The offensive in the factories and in the public services to sweep away the Peronist groups that had connived with the fallen dictatorship and to re-establish a union movement capable of expressing, without political intermediaries, the will and the desires of the working class, was never launched. The 'Thirty-Two', under the name of 'Mesa coordenadora de los sindicatos democráticos', were rapidly paralysed by being drawn into the political game, by corporativist tendencies, and by the absence of an over-all union strategy. The FORA, an anarcho-syndicalist federation which, although it had for a long time been in the forefront of workers' struggles, emerged anaemic from clandestinity, refused to allow for the changes of attitude that had taken place and the extent to which social institutions had taken root, and dreamed only of a return to the forms of organisation and of action that had characterised the twenties.

In the background of these human and tactical considerations, however, there remained the fundamental fact that the industries and the proletariat of Buenos Aires were still under

Peronist influence. Consequently, the idea of reconstructing the CGT led to conflicting points of view. Those who still cherished fond hopes of conquest supported the idea of a vast effort directed at bringing to the attention of the workers the corruption which permeated Peronist organisation, the thousand and one rackets in which its leaders had been involved, the unbridled waste for which they had been responsible, the demagogic nature of philanthropic works of the Fundación Eva Perón type, and Perón's own profound contempt for the masses which acclaimed him. 'No effort has been made to educate the masses', complained Luis Danussi, a union veteran, to an assembly of typographical militants. 'No attempt at raising the really significant issues, no pamphlets, no studies that would enable the workers to form a true opinion of the nature of Peronist corporativism.'

Danussi does not believe that the union movement can be put on its feet again by means of manoeuvres and by coming to terms with those who had attempted to destroy the Argentine union movement and who put the workers at the mercy of Perón's demagagy:

By accepting to co-operate with Peronist leaders within a CGT based on artifice and compromise without at the same time carrying out the necessary task of eradicating ignorance, democratic union leaders of all affiliations are contributing towards the perpetuation of the Peronist myth. Peronism only exists by virtue of its union apparatus. When Frondizi attempted to eliminate Peronism at the political level while yielding to it as far as the labour movement was concerned, all he succeeded in doing was to render still more political the organisations led by Peronists. These leaders hold power by virtue, not of their militancy on behalf of the working class, but of their loyalty to Perón. Without the investiture of their exiled leader they have at best the possibility of bringing together a minority of voters. Experience has shown that it is not the value of the work they do on behalf of the union but their use of the Peronist mystique that determines their success or failure in union elections. What is certain, however, is that one should not attempt simply to replace one mystique with another ideological fabrication. The only way of freeing the unions from Peronist influence is by using methods which would permit members to participate in the running of their organisation and to face squarely their responsibility as regards social and economic questions.[4]

The independent leaders who participated in the CGT did not share this opinion. Riego Rivas, who until the 1963 congress represented, together with a delegate from Fraternidad, the democratic tendency against the two representatives of the 'Sixty-Two', employed an entirely different language.

Since the liberating revolution, the Peronist unions have had to enter real union life and no longer be content with transmitting orders from the centre. The need to defend a certain number of advantages against the management forces the Peronist groups to act as union men. Their leaderships have for the most part been renewed, both because the most prominent Peronists have gone into exile or withdrawn into the shadows, and also because an initiative from below has purged the unions of their most corrupt elements. Admittedly, the 'Sixty-Two' line is dictated by Juan Perón, but one should also realise that many Peronist leaders prefer to have Perón in Spain rather than in Argentina. The *caudillo* can dismiss less easily when this has to be done by correspondence. And the very conditions of union life are conducive to more normal union behaviour.[5]

Rivas insisted on the goals that had been defined by the independents for a common strategy: 'The guidance of the national economy so as to reflect union policy; the task of workers' cultural and political education; and a complete democratisation of political life.'

This draft of a union policy is still very vague. Argentina's union leaders recognise that they still have to improvise and to manoeuvre continually if they are to avoid the perils of chaos. There are no union information bulletins, no union journals, no study centres, not even any study groups. In the vast CGT building at the end of Paseo Colón, near the ministries and on the fringes of the working-class districts, the staff is small, activities are confined to committee meetings, and the luxurious offices with their leather armchairs are for the most part empty.

Since going into opposition, the Peronist unions have struggled hard in order to survive the disappearance of the régime that had created them. They achieved this by using all the resources of the Peronist organisational law that the first provisional governments had hardly modified and that had been applied, to their advantage, by the Frondizi government. This law and its complementary provisions oblige the employer to charge union dues and to transfer them to the unions which have juridical existence. In other words, one single union is officially permitted by the state to negotiate on behalf of the workers and to represent them in the labour courts; and one single union automatically receives the dues, deducted at source. A worker can ask not to pay his dues. But this not only marks him out as a nonconformist: it also deprives him of a certain number of advantages—social benefits, for example—whose distribution is in the hands of the union. Creating another union presents enormous difficulties, for until it has won a majority in elections it can receive no dues via the firm, and has to depend on those voluntarily and directly contributed by rebels who have opted out of the established union. These peculiar characteristics of the union structure set up by the Peronist régime offer obvious advantages to whatever leaders control them, independently of their political affiliations, but restrain and even paralyse any internal forces of change and ensure the persistence of the leading group.

Needless to say, the arguments that have been put forward to attack this state of affairs do not all spring from the workers. The employers, too, have an interest in rendering the unions less monolithic. But the fact remains that under the present system considerable resources provided by the workers are manipulated by cliques subject to no control; and the social benefits themselves—medical services, co-operative chemists, holiday camps, etc.—are factors that act to keep the leaders in office by virtue of the fact that it is they who control their distribution.

With few exceptions, the career unionist has replaced the militant, and the conquest of an organisation has become the dream of a large number of *vivos*, of cunning individuals. The leadership of a union not only represents considerable public power: it is also remunerative, and in addition offers opportunities for rackets and embezzlement. A type of union gangsterism on North American lines has come into being. The Argentine Hoffas, however, are ineffective in defending their members. They are not the marginal profiteers of general prosperity, but the parasites of an impoverished economy. Consequently, the return to certain moral values, which is advocated by militants who have remained faithful to their vocation, encounters the obstacles of a partially integrated union structure and an atmosphere of widespread corruption. Although moral arguments carry little weight among the Peronist rank and file—where one can still find formulas like *Atorrante y ladrón, queremos a Perón* ('He may be a scoundrel, he may be a thief, but we want Perón') —trafficking and corruption are not peculiar to the Peronists. The democratic sector is itself largely contaminated. Enormous difficulties are encountered by 'European' groups, like the Social Democrats, which seek to create a new leadership and cleanse the union movement by the injection of younger, uncorrupted, elements. They act from the outside and are small groups with no roots in the reality of the shop floor. The best of them may end up as civil servants in the Ministry of Labour or in peripheral positions.

Is the attempt to win over the Peronist masses, outlined shortly after the fall of his régime and almost immediately abandoned, inconceivable and doomed to failure? Contacts with industrial workers do not suggest a simple answer. The main obstacle is the habit of the new workers in the more modern industries to remain as elements of a mass in search of security. They feel no responsibility and no desire to intervene. One might admit the possibility that a highly centralised organisation, able to create a mystique and carry out continual agitation on a wide front, might hope to capture a social stratum which behaves more like a mob than a class. But it seems unrealistic that small left-wing organisations made up for the most part of intellectuals—avant-garde Socialists, Trotskyists, nationalist revolutionaries—should hope to be able to do so. In the context of social forces, these little groups in ferment seem no more than gadflies, and their complicated reasoning leads in the end to advising the workers to vote for the Peronists. The interpretation and understanding of this tactic is a privilege of their leaders, whose behaviour seems explicable not in terms of sociology but, rather, of psychiatry. The gist of their argument seems to be that they see in the Peronist mass the motor of a possible revolution which they would lead. One Peronist leader commented, aptly, when one of these groups founded a journal called *Praxis*: 'It is the newspaper of workers learned in Greek.'

Despite a strange myth to the contrary held by the Peronists and various revolutionary circles, as well as by an important proportion of the anti-Peronist organisations, the Peronist unions have never, since Perón's departure in 1955, represented a real threat to the new régime. Their rôle has been to provide a legal framework for various outlawed Peronist movements and to mobilise votes in favour of the disguised representatives or occasional allies of their exiled leader.

In terms of workers' agitation in the true sense of the word, the leaders of the 'Sixty-Two' have not carried out any campaign in the hope of seeing it succeed. The widely publicised 'revolutionary' mobilisations were instruments in political manoeuvres and were concluded by clandestine negotiation. The general strikes in May 1962, despite the participation of independent groups, were no more than ceremonies. No forces were deployed in the streets, there was no show of strength. The famous 'battle plan' of 1964, which foresaw the taking over of factories, proclaimed 'a state of rebellion on the part of Argentina's workers' and was supposed to culminate in 'the total and simultaneous occupation of work-places throughout the country', was in marked contrast with the demands that were made. These corresponded to a memorandum presented to the president in December 1963, most of whose points had already been included in the government's programme. There was, indeed, the symbolic occupation of a few factories, but this came to an end when the local police superintendent intervened. It was only in June 1964 that a wave of small strikes was launched, more violent and with a few struggles, but they soon came to an end. A man like Andrés Framini, leader of the textile-workers' union, can scarcely control his own organisation. He tends to resolve conflicts in a personal way. Yet Perón's support at the time of elections for Greater Buenos Aires in 1962 was worth several hundred thousand votes for him.

All these considerations regarding union structure, which are nourished as much by nostalgia as by hope, will doubtlessly be outdated by the rising of a new generation. While attention is focussed on the acts and statements of the exiled leader in Madrid, and each provincial or general election leads to speculation on the part of strategists and tacticians, a slow transformation, related to the functioning of the organisations themselves, is taking place in Argentine union life. A new type of union personnel is taking office, more concerned with social services than with political polemics. Even within the sector that is still considered to be Peronist, a new trend can be discerned, centred upon the steelworkers' leader Augusto Vandor, in favour of integrating the present system. And on the independent side, where ideology is becoming progressively less and less influential, a similar trend is becoming apparent. The national leaders, the secretaries of the federations, those responsible for specialised departments and the official spokesmen of the main unions, are discovering that their function is neither that of militants expressing and reflecting the wishes of their electors nor that of personnel in the social service ministries, but that of specialists ensuring a liaison between important segments of society. Their position and their influence are favourable to the normalisation of post-Peronist institutions in Argentina. Despite the different shades of their political sympathies and origins, they are more and more coming to resemble a unified administrative staff.

An analysis of the composition of the vast population of Buenos Aires would probably lead to a more satisfactory explanation of the apathy of the masses than that given by many ponderous sociological frameworks. Direct observation of daily life can likewise contribute to understanding the attitudes of the *porteño*,* who always seems to be a bird of passage in his city, and to explaining why this mass in the process of becoming homogeneous does not feel that it belongs to a community.

While he is wielding his clippers, the barber is learning about conditions in Italian towns. He receives letters and reads magazines; he begins to compare prices, salaries and working conditions. He was born here, but his family environment has remained Italian. His father and mother used to tell him about the miserable conditions in their town before they emigrated. They used also to tell him those thousand and one insignificant details that constitute one's memories and create a nostalgia.

*i.e., inhabitant of Buenos Aires.

And so the barber thinks of emigrating too, but in the opposite direction. It is not that he is short of work, or badly housed. He just doesn't feel attached to Argentina. Italy today, or so it seems (he'd have to find out more about it before taking a decision) is an active, developing country where one lives better than one used to do. What he will do is to take two or three months' holiday to go and see for himself. He will go back to the family, observe and compare, and maybe remain.

This is not an isolated example. Noting the standard of living in Argentina, the Ministry of Finance has realised that the European labourer is no longer emigrating. His living standard at home is as high, or higher, than in Argentina. This is partially true. The Spaniard or the Italian from the poor areas no longer undertakes the long journey for the simple reason that industrial Europe can offer him what he lacks: work. The once nearly magical attraction of the Plate countries has disappeared. Nobody any longer comes to Buenos Aires in the hope of 'making America'. At best one can make a living here. This cook, for example, who expertly arranges with the tip of his knife the slices of meat, the braided tripes and the black pudding he will grill over a wood fire, in the purest *gaucho* style, turns out to be a Pole who arrived over thirty years ago. He does not think of returning: 'Here there's work and enough to eat.' It is the haunting memory of days in his native land without bread, of cold nights and empty factories, that keeps him here.

The dense crowds of Buenos Aires and its endless suburbs are largely made up of these recent or earlier immigrants who have arrived in waves, the remnants of European dramas stranded on the American side of the Atlantic. The collective adventures of races or peoples and the political or social adventures of individuals have ended in the plunge into the anonymous mass of Greater Buenos Aires. At the beginning of the First World War, there were 400,000 foreigners as against 120,000 'natives' in the capital alone, which was still a middle-sized town. Admittedly, the foreigners settle down and raise a family, and their children are Argentine. Nevertheless, in 1947, Buenos Aires still had 430,000 foreigners as against 615,000 Argentines. There is a continual melting down. This university professor, for example, had an Italian mother and a French father, and his wife is of Austrian descent. That union secretary's mother was German and his father Spanish; he married an English girl and his two Argentine sons have married an Italian girl and a Spanish girl respectively.

All that remains to bring together this mass with no common origin or traditions is a certain style of life imposed by the city. There are, however, little cells that resist atomisation. These are the smallest minorities, those characterised by a racial origin, a religion or a common experience which makes them virtually impermeable. These are the Armenians, the Basques, the Orthodox Greeks, the Spanish Republicans.

Then there has been the sudden growth of the capital and the great thrust of the rural populations towards the city. As from 1943, industrial production overtook the production of the *campo* (agriculture and cattle-rearing) which had been the traditional support of the Argentine economy. In an irresistible flood of internal migration, the *cabecitas negras* ('little black-heads') of the northern provinces—Salta, Tucumán, Santiago del Estero, Corrientes—attracted by high wages, invaded the capital and took over the ring of small towns surrounding Buenos Aires until they became vast outskirts. The statistical curves became almost vertical, with 5, 6, 7, maybe 8 million inhabitants in Greater Buenos Aires. Nor is the movement over. Other waves of immigrants are coming in. Tens of thousands of Paraguayans have come to swell the northern provinces or settle down around the capital. Chileans are filtering in to the west. Often illegally and for low wages, they come to sign on in the mines of Patagonia or in the industrial centres near the Cordillera. There are already other Chilean colonies at Mar del Plata on the Atlantic. At the gates of Buenos Aires whole populations are encamped, waiting to come in. Beyond the Riachuelo, whole villages of shacks, of *ranchos*, bear witness to the continuity of this tentacular movement. In these *villas miserias*, hidden by a long wall (built by Perón at the time of President Truman's visit) from the eyes of tourists, it is not wise to be too curious. It is a closed world that rules itself. But the prudish wall is covered with Peronist slogans.

One cannot understand the Peronist phenomenon without taking into account the rush to the city and industrial expansion. The institutions, the parties, the union organisations and the parliamentary rules of the game were unable to cope with the rapid transformation of the old Argentina, where 'the cow was queen', into a new Argentina with a thousand problems. 'In 1946', a democratic leader confessed: 'we were convinced that the front of democratic organisations would overcome the Peronist formula. We were badly defeated. Closed in as we were in the framework of our habits and putting too much trust in the value of a parliamentary régime, we underestimated the power of the new populations who did not participate in our political game and were frequently ignorant of it.'[6] Perón's skill lay in his focus on the *bárbaros*, on the *descamisados* who were new to the old institutions and organisations. Ever since the catastrophic earthquake in San Juan in 1943, he had skilfully organised the campaign of solidarity with the victims. From his position as Secretary of State at the Ministry of Labour and Social Security, he offered hundreds of thousands of men and women new to the city his powerful protection. He exalted their strength and magnified their rôle. Thus, by his constant mobilisation of popular pressures, he obtained a supplementary source of power which was to give a particular character to his playing of the classical rôle of *caudillo*.

One must, however, emphasise that Peronism, despite its style of government, its demagogy and its rudimentary ideology, did not effect any radical transformation in the functioning of the old institutions and he did not succeed—supposing that to have been his ambition—in installing a totalitarian régime. The lawyers and the soldiers continued to occupy the leading positions. Labour leaders were admitted, and they were few in number, only to subordinate positions, for the sake of appearances. The administration was, admittedly, invaded by the faithful, but this *clientela* was recruited from the same social strata and possessed the same university degrees as had its predecessor. The actual functioning of the administration was not changed. Perón did not alter the property system and left intact the power of large fortunes. An industrial bourgeoisie came into being and made terms with the régime. Strong men created the new dynasties which, without much difficulty, were to survive the fall of the régime. The names of Jorge Antonio and Rogelio Frigerio acquired a certain degree of celebrity as a result of their skill in public relations, the former as a captain of industry at the time of Perón, the latter as big business' *deus ex machine* under Frondizi.

It was specifically in the field of union organisation that totalitarian measures were applied, almost certainly because this sector contained possible supercessors of those in power and a potential for intervention more threatening to the 'system' than the group of politicians trained in the old school. But although the working-class populations were mobilised, they were not integrated into new structures. Thus, when economic and financial forces turned against him, Perón neither resorted to arming the masses nor did he attempt to impose totalitarian measures on society as a whole in order to preserve his power. Military intervention and the pressure of a significant element of public opinion—the two traditional factors in Latin American politics—were sufficient to provoke his downfall.

Industrialisation, urbanisation and their problems are factors which can explain the Peronist Justicialist phenomenon. Likewise, Argentine's wealth in terms of foreign exchange immediately following the Second World War and its privileged position as an exporter of foodstuffs to a shattered Europe, provide reasons for the survival of a régime whose economic policies were frequently insane. One must also recognise that even before Perón, and perhaps even more so afterwards, institutions and organisations no longer corresponded to the nature and the problems of the new Argentina. A proof of this can be found in the fact that the reform of the political parties is constantly on the agenda and that the working-class suburbs remain attached to the Peronist myth. The country lacks a solid and efficient administration to cope with the growth of the cities. It lacks public services able to transport, house and protect an even more compact urban population. There is no party which can bring together these millions of isolated individuals and offer them a means of participation. There are no hopes that can give them the necessary faith.

The organisations which exploit Peronist nostalgia and myth* do not put forward a radical programme. Violence occurs only in speeches and writings. The Peronist press and public speakers criticise the present policies of the military leaders, but maintain a solid respect for the army as an institution. They accuse the monopolies and international organisations of every crime, but extol private property. They are fiercely critical of the left-wing clergy, but seize every possible opportunity of expressing their loyalty to the Church. The Justicialista groups adopt totalitarian methods only in order to flatter the masses and to capture and exploit their anxieties. To break the resistance of the university and the student movements, they organised workers' demonstrations and cries of *Alpargatas sí, libros no* ('sandals yes, books no'). In the same spirit they froze teachers' salaries despite the rise in prices, and granted wage increases to factory workers. Even today this propaganda penetrates and influences the helpless masses who are anxious for security and whose desire for a strong government is evident. Surveys

*The Post Office sometimes receives letters addressed to 'Eva Perón, in heaven', begging her to intervene and solve problems of rent or hospital expenses.

reveal that two-thirds of the working-class population shares this attitude.

Nor is there any network of organisations which would allow the population to meet, to discuss and to play an active part in society. Less than 2 per cent of the adult population of Argentina participates effectively in party political life. Atomisation is complete. Even neighbourhood life seems to be absent. The crowds, forever passive, gather only for sporting events. This multitude of solitary individuals gives Buenos Aires an atmosphere of anguish. Men push, their shoulders forward, never giving way, oblivious of the others. The relations between the ticket-seller and the public are impersonal and anonymous. Only the family remains alive.

It is the family which ensures a certain mental equilibrium and permits income and expenditure within the solidary group to be maintained. The population lives under continuous inflation. Delays in the payment of wages and salaries and the constant increase in prices would provoke crises elsewhere, but here the effects are cushioned by a system of generalised credit thanks to which tradesmen and consumers mysteriously maintain a balance. One buys not only radio and television on credit but also shoes and groceries. Loans, postponements of payment, various arrangements and even usury are part of everyday life. And yet food remains plentiful; there is as yet no threat to the traditional peasant *puchero* (stew) or to the famous steaks.

The problems of the immense majority are those of a metropolis which has suddenly outgrown its public services. Housing is a problem, at any rate for those unable to pay exorbitant prices. Urban transport, which used to be quick and frequent, now suffers from outdated and not easily replaceable equipment. The railways, even the suburban lines of Buenos Aires, are mostly unreliable as regards timetables and totally so as regards comfort. Postal services operate only in so far as the personnel is paid on time, which is exceptional.

This situation has existed for so long that the inhabitant of Buenos Aires seems to have got used to it. Recriminations are useless: the only solution is to suffer, to consent and to adapt. No protest or outburst disturbs this lukewarm discipline. He knows and feels that he is alone. Political and financial scandals, concerning even the Banco de la Nación, the provincial administrations and the foreign-exchange markets, which he can read about in the press every morning, do not impel him to revolt. He is a dispassionate witness and a passive victim. He ends up by losing his faith in work and individual effort. He becomes more and more convinced that cunning—*viveza*—and good luck are the only ways of achieving success. He might vote for the party which promises to restore honesty in public life. He might, on the other hand, vote for the man who says he can restore order. Meanwhile, since one has to make a living, he will look for a supplementary job which will enable him to pay off a few debts and incur others. After all, as the Polish cook says: 'Here, there's work and enough to eat'.

4. *Chile: A Revolution without Revolutionaries*

Until recently the terms masses, *clientelae*, clans and promises were more appropriate to Chile than classes, parties, organisations and programmes. Chilean society does not possess a system of social stratification which makes political analysis easy. It is in the main an amorphous society.

Political leaders search for a hold over this mercurial material. They invent or borrow techniques of organisation to coagulate and order the fluid elements in a changing situation. They achieve no lasting success, for even the groupings they create are part of the same general phenomenon. They look instead for a method, an ideology or a faith which, while not depending on the national context, can still be grafted on to it.

No unsuspected crisis arrived to complicate the country's classic economic problems. By 1960, agricultural productivity was feeble, industry mediocre; mineral production was marginal to the national economy; the capital was overpopulated and there were insufficient outlets for an ever more abundant labour supply. Although no pressures of any particular intensity came from any given social class, it had become painfully obvious that Chile needed profound reforms and a serious reorganisation of society if these difficulties were not to lead to catastrophe.

No effort of any importance had been made by the traditional political formations either to discover the extent of the new problems or to devise commensurate solutions. The right-wing parties were mere electoral machines with no programme beyond maintaining the social status quo, and no doctrine apart from the classical 'respect for the established order', 'administrative integrity' and 'a balanced budget'. They were ruled by committees controlling considerable financial resources. Their supporters were candidates for political careers and manipulation, younger sons of important families or specialists in the parliamentary game, but when it came to defining or giving direction to the party's policy they fell back on generalities. Only months intervened between their being in office and their disintegration. The Liberals and Conservatives, whom as far back as 1852 Salvador Arcos the founder of the 'Sociedad de Igualdad', could barely tell apart,* did not even take the risk of playing the cards of the 'man on horseback' who was at hand, the descendant of Admiral Prat, and decided to form a new political organisation out of the débris left by their collapse.

After a century of existence, of struggles and of frequent triumphs, the Radical party by 1960 was beginning to experience the bitter-sweet effects of decadence. In an almost natural

*'One party is called *pipiolo*, or liberal, I don't know why; the other conservative, or *pelucón*. It certainly isn't because of any difference in political principles or convictions. It is not the views of their leaders that make the *pelucones* seem reactionary and the *pipiolos* liberal. But one should not forget that these *pelucones* are rich, make up the landowning caste, are privileged by education, accustomed to being respected and accustomed to despise the *roto*.' See Julio Cesar Jobet, *Los precursores del pensamiento social de Chile*, Editorial Universitaria, Santiago 1956.

way it stood for the interests of the petty bourgeoisie and of all those who longed to become part of this class. In Chile, this represented a considerable proportion of the population. It displayed the entire armoury of democratic ideas: anti-clericalism, social progress, state education, universal suffrage and social legislation. Its democratic nature implied, through its clubs and local associations, the participation of thousands of members. Corruption came in when the militant became a dispenser of offices and favours and the sympathiser became a client. The extent and the technical nature of the new problems became too much for traditional electoral politics. The available resources of an economy that was growing too slowly became insufficient to answer the demand for the public offices of which the Radical party had been one of the main dispensers. Hundreds of graduates and candidates for office jobs turned away from radicalism, not because of any ideological opposition but simply because the hundred-year-old party had nothing more to offer them. Its rôle as intermediary between the state and the individual citizen had been partly taken over by the coming into action of new parties which also claimed to be 'of the people'.

With its ability to restrain extremism and break through conservatism, the Radical party provided the necessary equilibrating mechanism during the period of economic development. Today, however, it is the economy itself which demands a new and imaginative stimulus, and this cannot be provided by a party of clients grown fat through frequent periods in office. During the previous one hundred years, the Conservative and Liberal parties had developed characters of their own: paternalist Catholicism in the former case, free enterprise and a neutral state administration in the latter. Both these conceptions of government presupposed the existence of a dynamic and responsible property-owning élite, whereas in fact this bourgeoisie made up of landowners and industries had displayed a spirit of enterprise only on rare and now distant occasions. The development of the country was achieved in large part by foreign immigrants—by Yugoslavs, Germans and Arabs—who, from a marginal position in society, succeeded in entering the ruling class. They took with them their fortunes but left behind their pioneering spirit.

The shortcomings of the ruling class eventually produced precisely what it had striven to avoid: the coming into being of state organisations in the economic sphere. In 1939, the Corporación de Fomento (CORFO) was founded so as to palliate the lack of initiative of the apathetic bourgeoisie. It has been responsible for some of the most important industrial undertakings, such as the Pacific Steel Company, the oil industry and the fishing industry. The engineers and technicians who, in 1960, drew up a ten-year development plan were in a dependent position as regards the law of free enterprise. At the time of the celebrations of CORFO's twenty-fifth anniversary, its general manager defined one of the corporation's tasks in the following terms: 'CORFO builds an enterprise, and when it is in full production transfers it to private ownership. With the proceeds of the sale we can begin further undertakings.'[7]

It is not surprising, therefore, to find that the younger generation of engineers and planners hesitate when the virtues of free capitalism are expounded to them and are tempted by ideologies which in effect give them a decisive social function. For with no other motor than a series of social tensions aggravated by the natural growth of the opposed elements, and according to pragmatic and short-term rules without plan or doctrine, Chilean society has changed. One has only to look at Santiago to see the extent to which change has taken place.

Without losing its characteristic appearance, the Chilean capital is growing and being transformed. The buildings in the centre grow higher and more massive every year, tunnelled through with commercial galleries. The city encroaches continually on to the plain. New residential districts, housing estates or 'mushroom towns'—the sad, ephemeral but continually recreated *poblaciones callampas*—stretch as far as the foothills of the imposing Cordillera. In a single generation, the population has doubled from 1 to approximately 2 million. But the *roto*, the classical proletarian, dressed like a scarecrow, unskilled, full of humour, progressing from submission to desperation to rebellion to success, is always there. Fewer in number than twenty years ago, not quite so shabby perhaps, less marked by the diseases and stigmas of misery—typhus, tuberculosis, alcoholism—less ready with the knife, less evident in the commercial heart of the city, the *rotos* still inhabit the older districts and are reproduced in the wood and corrugated-iron encampments which surround the city. There are fewer vagrant children, who at one time gathered in bands under the bridges and along the banks of the Mapocho, the mountain torrent whose waters carry the débris of Santiago. But there are still hundreds of shoe-shiners and children begging and wandering through the city after nightfall. The civil servants, commercial employees, petty bourgeois and other countless representatives of the middle classes have conquered and left their mark on parts of the city. But one can still see, in the older districts like those of the slaughter-house and the central market, groups of evangelists on rowdy and drunken Saturday nights, supported by feeble bands and calling out their confessions into the wind, calling on sinners to repent and seek the way of the Lord.

Faced with a transformed but not yet structured societys who can lay claim, not—any longer—to inheriting, but to replacing the bankrupt political leadership? Who can feel strong enough to achieve the parliamentary defeat of the Conservatives and Liberals and put an end to the system of privileges that they maintain?

Three parties are in the lists: a Communist party which has been there for forty years but which has never laid claim to power; a Socialist party made up of variegated and ill-assembled groups but which can reveal resourceful militants; and a Christian Democratic party which slowly took shape in opposition and which has suddenly been placed in power by its recent successes. Their vocabularies, their doctrinal formulations and their theoretical affiliations differentiate them. Their leaders are nevertheless similar in many respects and for the most part they belong to the intellectual petty bourgeoisie.

In a country where a party apparatus is a rare thing, the Chilean Communist party displays a clear superiority of organisation. A Communist parade or protest march is sufficient evidence of this. The *roto*, whose wit is urban but whose traditions are rural, is easily aroused but controlled with difficulty. Despite this, the party cells are able, for as long as the parade lasts, to guide and watch over him, thanks to a highly developed system of flank-guards, file-closers and leaders. When, on the anniversary of the Chinese Revolution, the activists of the Vanguardia Marxista Revolucionaria and the pro-Chinese Socialists organised two solidarity meetings in public halls, the leaders of the Communist party, to avoid the dangers of contagion, organised in forty-eight hours a large meeting to celebrate the Chinese people's victory, demanded the presence of all its cells and, in the person of its general secretary Luis Corvalán, launched a bitter attack on Peking's deviationists. The poet Pablo Neruda, forgetting his *Ode to Stalin*, then denounced the persecution of nonconformist Chinese intellectuals by Mao Tse-tung's police.

Having, most of them, held their positions since the disciplining of the Chilean party by the Latin American Secretariat of the International in the 1930s, the Communist leaders have followed and justified many turns and volte-faces in official doctrine. They have acquired the calm of old campaigners. They still remember Recabarrén, the party's founder, but have eliminated every trace of his unorthodox labourism. Their apparatus is sheltered and protected against initiative and spontaneous experiment. These tactics, however, are not favourable to securing roots for the Chilean Communist party. The exploitation of discontent among workers, peasants, civil servants and intellectuals for the sake of propaganda and putting up a front vis-à-vis the outside world does not lead to the creation of a solid organisation. Neither the union movement nor the vast potential of the peasantry is really under their control. The younger generation, in so far as it expresses its disquiet and follows a path other than that offered by the traditional parties, remains on the fringe of the party. Adolescents with an appetite for activism are rapidly disillusioned by the aridity and bureaucratic rigidity of party life. They turn instead to the dissident groups whose ideology differs little from the skilly served up by the Communist party, but where the barrack-room atmosphere is absent.

Despite its labourist vocabulary, the party is largely made up of and run by intellectuals. Its official daily, *El Siglo*, with a circulation of 20,000, consequently bears—particularly on Sundays—the appearance of a semi-literary, semi-political weekly.

The Socialist party, on the other hand, is more nervous, more sensitive, and less disciplined than its ally and rival. In an old surburban hall—a cinema during the week and a public meeting-place on Sunday mornings—the Chilean Socialist party is celebrating its thirty-first anniversary and introducing the new leaders of its youth movement, whose national congress has just ended. Several hundred men and women have gathered and are being warmed up by the songs of a group of young people in the gallery. They sing a *Marseillaise* with appropriate words, and then *Hijos del Pueblo*, the old Spanish Anarchist hymn, also adapted to the needs of the cause. The platform and the walls are decorated with red flags bearing the name of the affiliated sections and associations. Enormous cardboard letters in the proscenium spell out the name of the Socialist candidate for president:

ALLENDE. An artistic programme—Indian folk-music, a poetry reading, and a couple telling, in a few tableaux, the history of the party—is rapidly got through.

The party's technician, the man who runs its organisation, is Raúl Ampuero. He is an organisation man, and does not appear to have the support of numerous and well-disciplined cadres. The Socialist party has split and been stuck together again too many times since the 1930s for its militants to be united in doctrine or in battle. The memories of schisms and secessions are still fresh. Not so long ago, when General Ibáñez was giving his dictatorial régime a demagogic character, Ampuero was in favour of supporting the soldier-president while Allende opposed him. Both spoke for a party which claimed to be Socialist. Even today, Allende's entourage is made up of the Socialists whose ideas are closest to those of the Communist party, whereas Ampuero dreams of a centralised party, its rival in organisational efficiency and in its ability to mobilise the masses. Not a month passes without some militant or local association breaking away from the party, either for tactical reasons or as a protest against the strong hand of the secretariat.

The Socialist press is poor and ill-controlled. The journal *Arauco*, supposed to appear monthly, publishes material widely divergent in inspiration and tendency. In it one finds a nostalgia for the ideas of Jaurès, articles showing the influences of Castro, Tito and, until his fall, Ben Bella. The economics section brings together articles following the Sweezy-Huberman approach and others by ECLA planners. Another journal, *Izquierda*, is more uniformly impregnated with Fidelist phraseology, aggressive anti-Americanism and verbal extremism. The pro-Allende daily, *Última Hora*, is closer to being a vehicle of electoral propaganda than a journal reflecting a policy and run by a political organisation.

Ampuero's efforts, then, are directed towards the creation of an apparatus and not towards wielding a pre-existing organisation. The national congress of the Socialist party held in Concepción in March 1964 ensured his triumph, but only after the previous elimination of extreme left-wing groups, such as the pro-Chinese and the inevitable Trotskyists. This congress left one with the impression that Ampuero had succeeded in creating an apparatus with which to dominate the party but had not yet created a party apparatus.

Christian Democracy was born in 1957 after a recession from the old Conservative party. Its creators were mainly young militants, and it has gathered strength slowly. Except for a few occasions, power was not even remotely within its grasp. Hardened by opposition, it patiently forged its cadres, developed a network of activists and created specialist teams corresponding to the different sectors of public opinion.

It is only in the last few years that the Christian Democrat party has become an important political force. Its spectacular successes in the 1963 municipal elections placed it at the head of the Chilean political parties. Thenceforth, the hierarchy supported it in terms which were barely veiled by ecclesiastical language. In a course of lectures given to the students of the Catholic University of Valparaíso at the beginning of April 1964, Cardinal Raúl Silva Henríquez used a formula already fashionable in Italy and advised Catholics to give their support to those who are 'democratic in spirit and Christian in inspiration'.

Nor did this important support take the form only of general suggestions. For several years, a solid programme of research and organisation has been carried out by several centres. Most of them are run by Father Roger Vekemans. A Jesuit of Belgian descent, dynamic, imaginative and completely unhypocritical, Vekemans is the son of a Socialist militant. Some of the finest minds in Chile, organised into teams, are analysing social situations and problems, preparing long- and short-term solutions, and drawing up an economic policy. Many are not Catholics. Teachers, sociologists and economists are co-operating in this pioneering programme simply because it is one of the first attempts ever made to attack the country's problems in all their complexity. The results of this patient research have slowly penetrated political and corporate organisations. Christian Democracy has become the majority tendency in some student movements. It controls a large number of munici-palities, has an influence on professional associations, and is attempting to penetrate the unions and the peasant areas. It is a leading force among those concerned with protecting the *publaciones callampas*.

Yet the presence of Christian Democracy among the masses does not mean an identification with them. The party's orators go among them and are sympathetically received. But the large gatherings of militants in Santiago reveal that members of the middle class, commercial employees, civil servants and profes-sionals still make up its backbone. Like the Communist and the Socialist parties, Christian Democracy has thus far not succeeded in harnessing the energies of the workers and the peasants.

A massive wave of opinion in favour of change took the Christian Democrat candidate, Eduardo Frei Montalva, to the presidency in 1964. He put forward a fairly precise reformist programme, which included measures to ensure greater control and efficiency in the mining industry, a reorganisation of agriculture at the expense of the inactive or unproductive landowners, tax reform and some measures aimed at improving housing conditions. The evening after his triumph on September 4, 1964, an enthusiastic crowd chanted two particularly signifi-cant slogans: *Chile es y será un país de libertad* ('Chile is and will remain a country of freedom') and *Revolución sin paredón* ('Revolution without firing squads').

The supporters of the Christian Democrats and of FRAP (the Socialist-Communist coalition) all expressed the hope of being able to break away from the past and its inheritance of vested interests and rigid attitudes. But what forces were there able to bring this hope to fruition? The Christian Democrats

157

have chosen the way of 'revolution within legality'. In other words, they hope to work within the normal parliamentary framework. This implies that they do not wish, do not dare or do not know how, to make use of the popular pressure which they nevertheless helped to bring into being during the two years of their electoral campaign.

Not only the oligarchy, but also the opposition, which claimed to be more 'revolutionary' and more 'reformist' than the new government, were to use all the means of the institutional framework to block Frei's programme. In addition, his adversaries were to use other means at their disposal. Landowners broke up their estates among members of their families; and FRAP organised strikes among the workers. For their own part, the Christian Democrats have walled themselves in with their own victory by trying to work only with their supporters. They have not attempted to bring in the large number of technicians and specialists who supported other candidates but who remain nevertheless in sympathy with the government's programme of reforms.

The changes that were desired by the majority cannot, therefore, be put into effect until they have passed through the long complications of parliamentary procedure. These changes will be attempted by a party which has at its disposal neither the means of large-scale propaganda—the press, radio, television —nor a mass organisation. Nor does this party, brought to power by the will of the majority, have the support of a victorious social class, either of an enterprising bourgeoisie or of an organised proletariat. All it has at its disposal are its numerous teams of supporters whose perception of the problems to be faced and whose ambitions for future posts rather than for the mediocre sinecures of the past differentiate them from the remaining mass of the middle class.

Some leaders of the Christian Democrats had foreseen this possibility. The day after his election, Frei stated clearly in an interview the difficulties that lay ahead.

It will clearly be very difficult to stimulate the creation of an organic popular basis for our democracy without the active participation of the state. In Chile there does not exist a vigorous basic structure. Consequently, for the first stage at least, the state must give an impetus to this vast movement whose goal is to make the country democratic. Given this end, the best conditions of development are those of an interplay of tension and collaboration between the state and the pressure groups. On the one hand, the state will foster the consolidation of these groups; on the other hand, they will be given legal status so that they can come to have an existence of their own, independent of the state's direct intervention. Our conception of social democracy tends to make the higher organisms of the state a product of the basic popular organisations. What is essential in this policy is to avoid the formation of paternalist or *étatiste* structures.[8]

It would appear that the Christian Democrat 'commandos' who specialised in the problems of popular organisation harboured illusions as to the ease with which they would be able to supplant the influence of the Communist and Socialist parties, particularly in the trade unions. At first, they respected the rules of an established game. Like their Socialist and Communist rivals, they created groups aimed at gaining control of the unions. They had little success, since the other groups were experienced in organisation politics. More serious, however, was the fact that these tactics prevented them from putting forward and implementing the idea of a truly independent union movement, no longer a simple branch of the national parties, and able to play a key rôle. The Christian Democrat 'organisers' were seldom militants trained on the shop floor. They were, rather, intellectuals charged with specific tasks, or workers who foresaw the possibilities of union action on a party, and no longer a factory, basis. The euphoria of the campaign led them to confuse the world of propaganda and ideas with that of everyday life and the problems of work. Their triumphs at the polls, in the working-class districts or in the slums, found few echoes in the sphere of the permanent organisations.

The Chilean trade-union movement, which consists mainly of the Central Única de los Trabajadores (cut), is in fact poorly supported. Its membership is split between white-collar workers and manual labourers, and its few organised clusters are corporativist in spirit. The cut itself, which claims to have 300,000 members, has in fact only half that number, and most of these do not pay dues to the federation. It acts with a great show of slogans but has only a feeble control over its constituent organisations.

As for the agricultural labourers and peasants, no systematic and long-term attempt has ever been made to organise them. Even the pre-war Popular Front did not dare to reach out into the field of agriculture and did not allow the unionisation of agricultural labourers. This is doubtlessly the reason why the Christian Democrats seriously hope to establish a firm basis in the rural areas by means of the associations and co-operatives that will be made necessary by the land reform.

These considerations bring to light a fact that is usually neglected. The struggle against the past and tradition not only has to face the resistance of the oligarchic interests and of apathetic industrialists; it must equally come up against the groups of wage-earners who, by labour struggles, by their peculiar situation in the economy or the state organisations and by their electoral weight, have succeeded in obtaining for themselves corporate privileges whose short-term defence is easily confused with the maintenance of the status quo.

5. *Bolivia: From Militia to Army*
Until 1952, the landowning and mining interests controlled the main sources of wealth in Bolivia. The Indian population (55 per cent of the whole) lived in conditions of near-serfdom, tied to the land on the high plateaux or in the valleys, and

participating in society only as a source of agricultural labour-power. An élite of Spanish descent provided the governmental and administrative personnel of the provinces and the towns. The *mestizos* (nearly a third of the population) on the fringe of the Indian masses, performed in the towns and cities the rôle of a petty bourgeoisie. They engaged in commerce at the local level and were low-grade civil servants. They played a part in political life and furnished the troops for electoral battles and street demonstrations. Slowly they became the political class whose expression is the Movimiento Nacional Revolutionario.

The MNR won the 1952 elections, but the traditional power-groups, together with the agrarian and mining interests, tried to wipe out this victory with violence. The *rosca** fought its last battle and was crushed by a popular movement made up of Indians and *mestizos*. The popular nature of the 1952 revolution found expression in immediate social measures. The estates were occupied and broken up. In the mining centres and rural communities, a militia was created and provided with heterogeneous arms. The power-centres of the official party were largely influenced by peasant action and by the existence of local centres of power. The MNR recognised and gave legal sanction to the land reform that had been spontaneously carried out, thus ensuring the support of the Indian population. It nationalised the mines, which were the main source of the national income, but soon found itself split between two groups. One group saw in nationalisation a means of ensuring the state a supply of foreign exchange which would permit the planning of the economy and the establishment of a vast party bureaucracy. The other group claimed to speak for the miners and wanted them to be represented in the government.

In the pamphlets put out by the Central Obrera Boliviana (COB), one finds constantly reiterated the thesis that the Bolivian

*The Bolivian term for the defenders and beneficiaries of the oligarchic groups, the landowners and the tin 'barons'.

revolution was the result of the efforts of the peasants, of the workers and of the petty bourgeoisie, and that consequently the trade unions should be not an autonomous force but one member of an alliance which would be reflected in the composition of the government. One can find here a certain Trotskyist vocabulary, but the 'left' of the MNR, headed by Juan Lechín, the miners' leader, appropriated it for itself. This idea has its attractions for those who are bewitched by politics and the mechanisms of power, but it implies that the union movement should be subject to government policy and that the COB should not organise with a view to claiming control over the industrial sector.

The nationalisation of the mines was significant. An enormous bureaucracy, claiming to represent the revolutionary government but almost totally ignorant of the problems of mining, invaded the administration of the mines. The miners, who immediately after the revolution were prepared to make extra efforts and sacrifices, realised that these new administrators were technically useless and that their mistakes would mean wastage, inefficiency and extra work. The miners soon resorted to a corporative defence of the advantages they had already won. At the same time, the new managers and administrators in industry, who were unable to face the problems of labour administration and feared the reactions of the workers, gave way tremblingly whenever a workers' delegation presented itself, and thus they reinforced the power of local political organisations.

The 'mining' deputies could not propose any solution to the economic problems raised by the collapse of tin prices on the world market and the progressive deterioration in the quality of the ore, but nevertheless they continued to defend their *clientela*—both the miners and the superfluous administrators—as a whole and without discrimination.

The oversubtle political intelligentsia was soon to disguise a situation which was nonetheless apparent. The miners were put forward as being an essential element in the revolution, but they had no chance whatsoever of participating in the organisation of their own labour. This situation has become progressively worse and more evident over the years. Chaos and the bureaucratic inflation in the mines called for solutions which were neither labourist nor political. Foreign specialists and experts attached to groups which were prepared to invest capital proposed a general reorganisation as a precondition to any foreign aid. The Miners' Federation, whose leadership was involved in factional struggles within the MNR and had the support of the vice-president (and ambassador in Rome) Juan Lechín, found itself isolated. It had not put forward a policy for the mines, but was in a position to paralyse the functioning of the economy.

Although it had the support of the peasants, the government of Paz Estenssoro could not hope to break the miners' resistance without the use of force. Clashes between workers and peasants of the MNR became more frequent. Each side sought the support of the army to tip the balance. This was a new army, which had been created in the space of a few years, was linked to the régime, and progressively showed itself to be the only solid structure of the new state. It could not be long before it carried out the role of arbiter and exacted its price for so doing.

It was the fragmentation and powerlessness of the political formations that brought the army to the fore in the political scene. From 1962, both the Paz Estenssoro and the Juan Lechín factions of the MNR were seeking an alliance with Barrientos. In other words, both leaders sought military backing and in so doing admitted their own impotence. All that was left of the MNR movement were rival factions kept apart by dead bodies. The leaders of each controlled a region or a social group and had the support of a political clan, but neither of them could claim authority on a national basis. Furthermore, these local or occupational bases were frequently assured by organisations based on force and fear rather than by their ability to express democratically the will of the majority. Each clan had carved out a fief held by controlling a few key positions and by means of an armed militia either officially or unofficially maintained out of the local budget. In the capital itself, there flourished such groups maintained at the public expense: state or private police forces or Indian *campesinos* (peasants) who, finding no work in a nonexistent industry, had become soldiers or mercenaries. Elsewhere there were the peasant militias and, in the mining areas, the miners' militias.

Behind the fluid and interchangeable ideologies, there appears a new ruling class which is feeling a way towards establishing a more stable institutional framework in which to consolidate its privileges. Meanwhile, these new feudal lords attempt to preserve their domain and their troops so as to be in a strong position when it comes to naming the sovereign—whom they would like to see feeble if they cannot manipulate him directly.

The army is a young one. Until it became aware of its possible rôle, it was no more than the creation and dependant of the official party. It has at its disposal no more than approximately 10,000 men with which to cover a difficult and compartmented country which includes the high Andean plateaux and valleys as well as an immense tropical plain.

Despite this chaotic situation, we should not forget that the Bolivian revolution, whatever its misfortunes, was a considerable event with irreversible social consequences. The term *indio* has given way to that of *campesino*, and this is not simply a change of names. The first, and without a doubt the main, beneficiary of the revolution of April 1952 was the Indian peasant who yesterday was tied to the land which he did not own and was entirely subject to, and dependent on, the land-owners. Today he works his small plot, goes to the town, sells his produce, and sometimes undertakes the great adventure of going east.

Whether in the tiny open-air market where barter—dried

fruit for dehydrated potatoes—is still the rule, or in the local towns, the Indian cultivator is beginning to participate in commercial life. It is still not integration, however, and ECLA's statisticians are impatient at the sluggishness with which economic circuits between the towns and the rural centres are being established. The peasant is more often than not content with buying a few yards of cloth, a few shoddy goods and alcohol—too much alcohol. For the most part, he still lives in a closed economy. Yet, along the dusty roads that go from La Paz to Lake Titicaca, one can see a few bicycles and sometimes a motor scooter. The mechanical age is beginning to arrive. In the villages—some still built of *adobes* (dried mud blocks) others already smarter, with some whitewashed walls and every now and again a house with an upper storey—transistor radios are beginning to appear. Rural schoolteachers, religious orders and Protestant missions have opened schools, or, if a building is not available, they give lessons in the open air. Even if the women still preserve their traditional form of dress— woollen *mantas* with long fringes, bowler hats, ample and vividly-coloured skirts—the men are more and more coming to wear European clothes, not only in the capital but also in many parts of the *altiplano*. Another sign of the same trend is the fact that it is frequently the woman who works the land while the man goes to the town. Indian society, static until ten or twelve years ago, is beginning to move, and this stirring provokes problems. The younger generation is attracted by the town, but does not always find a job. The stagnant economy and the non-existent or paralytic industries cannot absorb this new labour-force. There is thus the danger of the creation of a *lumpenproletariat*.

Many peasant families have moved in another direction, from the high plateaux to the valleys, and from the valleys to the tropical regions, to the Oriente, where land is to be had for the taking and where there are two harvests a year. This is an adventure for the man of the Andes who leaves his old habitat at 12,000 feet or more and moves down into the tropical valley, going from the potato to manioc and from corn to the banana. He sometimes even loses the need to chew *coca* leaves.

The Indian world has begun to move. This phenomenon cannot be included in the forecasts of statesmen, politicians and union leaders, nor can it be worked into an economic development plan. It has immediate and serious consequences. The commercial output of agricultural products falls, either because peasant consumption has increased or because certain extensive cultures have been abandoned, or for both these reasons. Furthermore, the proceeds which the peasant gets from the sale of his products are not spent in their entirety. The peasant tends to hoard, and this is another subject of lamentation for the economists. Until recently, the peasant population did not enter into economic statistics. Now it is beginning to enter the national economy in its own way, but nothing can yet be calculated. Whatever happens, and whatever the regrets that this unorthodox revolution may provoke among the theorists, the peasant is leaving behind him the colonial age and he is on his way.

With the elimination of the economic power of the old privileged class, a serious blow was dealt to the small white élite, proud of its Spanish origins. In towns like Tarija, with its Andalusian tradition, or Sucre, still remembering the days when it was the capital, one can still see, on Sunday mornings before Mass, families gathered round their proud mother whose black hair is in bandeaux under her *mantilla*; and the housemaids follow the children wearing blouses and starched lace collars. This society is still alive, but with no resources other than those from a few old houses or apartments. It is now marginal. It has been pushed to one side by the rise of the new *mestizo* strata.

The *mestizo* has become mobile and is now a politician, a trade-union leader, or a peasant organiser. They are sometimes accused of making such-and-such a union or such-and-such a peasant district which they hold as a fief pay dearly for their influence. *Mestizo* support or disagreement is still important in the struggle between governmental factions. The influence of the *Mestizo* class is also beginning to be felt in urban commerce and in small industries, as well as in public administration. It does not have to fear the competition of the *campesino*, and the privileges of the old rulers have been swept away by the revolution. Its best card is education, its best weapon a university degree, its most promising field of action an administrative or political bureaucracy.

Linked to this social mobility is the movement that is attracting adolescents towards the schools, reading and knowledge. In Cochabamba, for instance, one can see, even before dawn, under the streetlamps and neon signs (domestic electricity has not yet been installed everywhere and is expensive) boys reading aloud with the utmost concentration. The public gardens, avenues and squares of Sucre are thronged by students deep in textbooks and notebooks. Generally poor, they seek the calm that they cannot find in a room shared with one or two other students, and buy page by page the duplicated lectures they cannot afford to buy complete. This desire for learning cannot be explained solely in terms of a desire to secure a more stable and better-paid employment than manual labour. In La Paz and Santa Cruz, as in Cochabamba, shoe-shiners and fruit- or cigarette-vendors can be seen practising their writing in small notebooks.

An Indian peasantry which is learning to be free, an internal migration that reveals the extent and diversity of Bolivia to its inhabitants, the rise of the *mestizos* to managerial posts, and a general rush towards the schools and the universities—these are some of the more pleasing and encouraging aspects of post-revolutionary Bolivia. But this alone is clearly not enough to make it a solidary and contented nation with a stable government. The revolution, the agrarian reform, the nationalisation of the mines and the rise of a new working class are all natural phenomena rather than measures arising out of the implementation of a programme.

6. *Cuba: Self-determination Reserved for the Leader*

The essays that have been produced to explain the structure of the new form of power that resulted from the 'Movimiento 26 de Julio' and from the fall of Batista's régime, even if they have not helped much in providing a definition of these phenomena, have at least discredited the stock political formulas of both left and right. For some, it has simply been a case of finding a single explanation for the birth, for the triumph and for the subsequent changes in *Castrismo*. The whole process is reduced to the problem of knowing whether Fidel Castro had been a Communist and Marxist from the outset of his political career. For others, it has been a case rather of inventing successive and contradictory pseudo-theoretical justifications for a complex process of social change whose internal logic could doubtless emerge from an analysis of Cuban society but which can never emerge from the accounts of intellectuals in search of revolutionary folklore.

The declarations of the Cuban leader do not help to explain the mechanisms of the changes that have taken place both in policy and in ultimate goals. In the process from the 'humanist' programme at the beginnings of the movement, to the 'liberty with bread and without terror' of the seizure of power and to the 'Marxism-Leninism' of the following years, there is neither continuity nor development of thought. There is, rather, a choice of slogans that would justify and make easier the struggle for power, its conquest and its organisation. The laborious ideological constructions of foreign partisans only follow, after a time-lag and with no real knowledge of the evolutions and transformations that have taken place, the phases of the coming to power of a new ruling stratum. Agreeable phrases about the 'peasant revolution', 'direct democracy' or the 'dictatorship of the proletariat' may reassure the believers, but they have little bearing on the doings of the régime in Havana.

The 'Movimiento 26 de Julio' was, right from the beginning, a movement formed, conceived of and functioning as a middle-class movement. The composition of the first governments after Batista's fall seems to confirm this. Among the eighteen members of the ministerial team, eight were lawyers, five were professors or students, three were university-trained professionals, and two were military men.* It was after the taking of power that the separation began to take place within the initial amalgam, following a line of cleavage that can be roughly traced as follows. On the one hand, there were those who had been integrated in society, or hoped to be able to become integrated; on the other, there were those who linked this future to a total restructuring of society and hoped to find a secure basis for their power that they could not find in society as it was previously.

Fairly rapidly, Castro eliminated the leaders and militants who had taken part in the activities against Batista in the hope of installing a democratic type of government and applying a non-dictatorial revolutionary policy, and those who opposed the progressively more marked trend towards personal power

*Theodore Draper, in *Castro's Revolution: Myths and Realities* (New York 1962) gives a list—compiled by a minister in spring 1960—of the members of the Cabinet and their ages. Osvaldo Dorticós, president, lawyer, 40; Fidel Castro, prime minister, lawyer, 33; Augusto Martínez Sánchez, Labour, lawyer, 34; Raúl Roa, Foreign Affairs, professor, 53; Osmany Cienfuegos, Public Works, architect, 31; Armando Hart, Education, lawyer, 29; Raúl Castro, War, student, 29; Raúl Cepero Bonilla, Commerce, lawyer, 29; Regino Boti, Economy, lawyer, 37; Rolando Díaz Astarain, Finance, captain (of marines), 35; Julío Camacho, Transport, commander, 34; Serafín Ruiz de Zárate, Health, doctor, 35; Pedro Miret, Agriculture, engineering student, 32; José Naranjo, Interior, medical student, 30; Raquel Pérez, Social Welfare, doctor in philosophy, 32; Enrique Oltuski, Communications, engineer, 29; Alfredo Yabur, Justice, lawyer, 35; Luis Buch, minister for the Presidency, lawyer, 47. Subsequent changes have not altered the social composition of the cabinet, which is still made up of professionals and intellectuals.

or the single party. In the rebel army, in the administration and in the Movement, men like Huber Matos, Felipe Pazos and Manuel Ray were opposed, imprisoned or forced into exile. And this differentiation does not only take place within the ruling groups. It is equally manifest in the stream of emigrants. During the first months, the emigrants were mostly those who supported or who benefited from the fallen régime; but later new waves began to leave the country, including tens of thousands of members of the middle classes and of workers, many of whom had been democratic revolutionaries during the anti-Batista period.

It is not pressure from the peasants and the workers which has provoked the hardening of the régime and the elimination of the 'luke-warm'. The new ruling group has its hands full in trying to control the unions and the peasants. It is not the triumph of proletarian demands which explains the new political emigration and the growth of opposition to the régime; on the contrary, it is the transformation of the popular grass-roots organisations into dependents of the central power, controlled and manipulated from above, that provokes the departure of all those who had hoped to build a freer and more just régime.

Programmes and attempts at social transformation do not spring from the desires and wishes of the working-class and peasant masses, nor are they based on their organisations. They correspond to the needs and perspectives of the new ruling class. Political power provides the temptation—which has shaken the country and taken it to the brink of collapse—to create an entirely new economy and administration shaped in the image of the centralised political power and at its disposal. Declarations about the end of monoculture, the clear transformation of the economy and industrialisation in two years, certainly correspond to the need to find a solution to the country's basic problems; but they also illustrate the desire to solve these problems from above, the central power being the only organism of decision-making, and to create a counter-society with no roots in the past, conceived and constructed from above.

These ideas may claim to be Socialist; but one of those who developed them, 'Che' Guevara, did not hide his profound contempt for the peasant whose only dream was to own a plot of land and for the worker who did not want to work on Sundays. The reinforcement of the power of the state, the elimination of the private sector in agriculture and the introduction of compulsory military service, correspond to the internal need of the new ruling class to concentrate all power in its hands and to shape the life of the nation. Difficulties and defeats, particularly in the economic sphere, do not lead to a relaxation but to a reinforcement of central discipline and control. Behind the confusion of interchangeable slogans, replaced doctrines, changes of perspectives and restructured alliances one can see the permanence of a political power that cannot be softened by political vocabularies.

This desire for power is the central phenomenon, for it survives all the reorientations and is unchanged by the most dramatic crises. The serpentine wanderings of the policy put forward by Fidel Castro seem to be no more than phases in a search for the means of creating, with no doctrinal guide and no historical precedent—and putting to good effect the enormous internal and external problems caused by the perfecting of the system—an apparatus of power coextensive with society.

Factional struggles between the Fidelist nucleus of the old 'Movimiento 26 de Julio' and independent groups within the same movement, or between the old guard and the younger generation of the Communist party, and the rivalry between the two main currents of opinion, can be interpreted, after five years of convulsions, as being expressions of the emergence of a ruling class. As Boris Goldenberg, a masterly observer, puts it: 'The new ruling class has not yet crystallised, while tens of thousands have risen into leading positions, most of them from the ranks of the lower classes or from among the formerly frustrated young intellectuals.'[9]

Popular pressures, oppositions of every kind, the grievances of any social group, the peasants' need of land, the desire for public liberties among the majority, the workers' hope for an efficient trade-union organisation—all these have naturally been instruments in the conquest of power. This amalgam of discontents and hopes created a majority movement which could overcome a dictatorial régime without any popular base. But this amalgam was no more than the sum of different sectors of the population with no common programme, whose immediate interests did not demand a complete restructuring of society. This situation was favourable to any government apparatus which could take over from Batista's machine, and offered exhilarating possibilities for the team of 'availables'.

The previously unstructured nature of Cuban society, the absence of a solidly established dominant class or of any class linked to an essential economic activity, made much easier the creation of an entirely new decision-making framework. But for this new structure to be established, a leader was needed who could bring together the forces of change and eliminate the supporters of the status quo and the organisations which thought themselves able to bring about change independently. The missing element was provided by the irrational, charismatic personality of Fidel Castro. Illogical decisions, absurd economic adventures and risky decisions in foreign politics do not provide a solution, even partially, to Cuba's problems, but they reinforce the importance of the leader as arbiter and contribute towards making him indispensable. The shortage of foodstuffs, one result of an economic policy drawn up by amateurs, leads to the creation of a new bureaucracy dependent for its existence on the régime—and hence faithful to it. On the other hand, since it is the victim of Castro's sarcasm, discontent is directed towards the bureaucracy and not against the régime.

In the period marked by the break with the United States and the surrender to the Soviet Union, the former seems to have been the decisive factor, not because it corresponds to a well-thought-out foreign policy, but simply because it freed Castro from a series of immediate constraints and limitations. The fact that the economy is now more narrowly subject than before to a world power, together with the fact that the decision to become involved in the struggle for world leadership between the two great blocs is a dangerous one, is not of decisive importance for Castro. The transfer of foreign-policy difficulties from a nearby power, which had for a long time been established in the island, to another but distant imperialist power contributed at the time to wipe out the past and to give the leader new opportunities to create an unconditionally faithful following and to make his personal presence even more indispensable.

The useless and indiscriminate declaration of war against all Latin American political régimes, and the repeated call to make the Andes a new Sierra Maestra, cannot be justified by an analysis of the real situation in the various regions of South America. They correspond, rather, to the needs of internal policy and to Castro's unbridled desire to break with the past completely and build a new world according to his own specifications.

The attitude of most of his opponents, and in particular of the émigrés who, fondly deluding themselves, identify with the United States, only makes his policy easier. For it is only with a realistic opposition policy conceived in terms of internal needs, events and problems which express the desires of the active sectors of Cuba's population and bring them to participate, that it would be possible to present an alternative to the present erratic but determined ruling group and demand the right of self-determination.

7. *Venezuela: When the Opportunities Come First*

Venezuela's situation is a paradoxical one. It suffers from most of the evils of underdevelopment, but its rate of economic growth has been one of the highest in the world for the last thirty years. It would therefore appear that, if economic development is an important factor in preventing social tensions and conflicts, in isolation it can do little. In fact, the extreme rapidity of the modernisation of an economy multiples conflicts. The old structures do not have time to change and adapt themselves to their new administrative and political tasks.

During the 1920s, Venezuela was one of the poorest and most backward countries in Latin America. Its social structure was traditional and relatively simple. A small ruling group of agrarian property-owners controlled exports, provided the ruling political personnel and accepted the protection granted it by the army and the dictator. Misery, exploitation and an extremely unequal distribution of income and life-styles between the rural population and the small privileged élite did not threaten the stability of the régime. There was as yet no way of channelling discontent and bringing it to bear on the political system.

The sudden arrival of wealth derived from oil in the 1930s acted as an irreversible revolutionary force. In the first place, this new industry did not arise from the will, the spirit of enterprise or the efforts of the oligarchy. The initiative, the capital and the experts were foreign. There was thus no progressive adaptation of the social classes and the state administration to a new situation. On the other hand, the financial irrigation of society and the need for local administrators connected with the oil companies, their management and the transport and construction they needed, contributed to the sudden development of a middle class whose political influence was soon to be felt.

During this period, the first democratic organisations, and

in particular Acción Democrática, came into being. Their influence was increased by the migration of the rural population to the cities. As early as 1945, they obtained a clear majority in the elections. The army and the old ruling groups carried out a successful coup d'état to prevent the great transformation of the social structure and of the political system, but were unable themselves to provide the administrators, the technicians and the political leaders that were required by the new society.

The middle class and the parties which represented it did not possess the qualified personnel necessary for the new industries, for the expanding urban centres, for the reorganisation of agriculture—which remained in the hands of the old and the very young—for the thousand and one organisations that are called into being by a modern state. But the posts were there, and the desire to fill them gave the middle classes the necessary enthusiasm. The state, which controlled the resources derived from the exploitation of oil, and dispensed credits and subsidies to create new industries or to put into effect the agrarian reform, to create or to modernise the entire economic infrastructure, and to catalogue and develop all the country's natural resources, had become the first entrepreneur and took the place of a non-existent bourgeoisie. Little of what remained of the ancien régime could be recovered and put to use. But the main elements of the old machine did still exist and could hamper the functioning of the new one. The man faced with this infinity of complex problems became more and more tempted to return to the recent past and to a simple and ordered, even if unjust and unequal, system.

Faced with the former of these dangers, President Betancourt's answer was to avoid making any threat against the clans and institutions inherited from the past. Thus privileges and prerogatives were safe and they had nothing to fear. What he wanted was simply time in which to build a modern Venezuela, with all the necessary institutions, administrations and industries, in the hope that once the new Venezuela had been created the old one of landowners and *coroneles* would crumble into dust. To a certain extent, Betancourt guaranteed that the ornaments of the ancien régime would not be touched, but at the same time he took care that they should not seek to play the leading rôles. This became clear when the flight of capital, with the amortisation of the heavy debts incurred during the dictatorship, threatened the stability of the financial system and of the régime itself. In 1959-60, the government took severe measures. Imports were restricted, exchange was controlled and sumptuary expenditure cut back. As a result, imports of goods and services, which in 1957 had amounted to $2,300,000,000, had fallen by 1961 to $1,360,000,000.

These tactics depended entirely on the president's skill and were directed at maintaining the original vigour of the reno-vation movement and keeping open the possibilities of fulfilling the hopes of the middle classes. To those who thought that the country should jump stages, crush by force the remnants of the past and try the Cuban way, Betancourt steadily offered participation in all its forms. Finally, when the last hope of left-wing terrorism lay in provoking a right-wing coup d'état, he showed himself the effective master of all the weapons conferred by power.

If the old ruling groups could not even partly provide the personnel for a nation that was changing, the working classes were equally unable to intervene by means of grass-roots organisations. At best, they could express their hopes at the polls and their preference for the new régime when it was in danger. Venezuelan democracy is being built from above and cannot rely either on the trade unions or on autonomous peasant associations or on an independent co-operative move-ment. The dependence of these organisations on the state, mainly through the political parties, is for the time being complete. This dependence can be explained, not only in terms of the state's need to create or foster organisations with which it can conduct a dialogue, but also in terms of its need to create social categories in order to give a certain degree of coherence and equilibrium to the new society. Thus, in certain rural areas, a peasantry has virtually had to be 'invented'.

In the region of Turmero, 100 kilometres to the west of Caracas, the land reform offers itself for inspection. As one leaves the dirt roads, frequently crossed by ditches filled with stagnant brown water, one comes across several rows of square houses, each surrounded by a border of naked soil. These houses, all made according to the same pattern, have been built with light but good-quality materials. Ventilation is ensured by a series of openings just below the roof which, even at night when the doors and windows are closed, helps make the tropical heat bearable. Electricity has been installed and there is running water. But, despite the modern architecture, this still feels like a traditional village of *chozas* (huts). Naked children run among the houses and along the road and mothers with coloured dresses and loud voices shout to each other from door to door.

Nearby are the five hectare ($12\frac{1}{2}$ acre) plots separated from one another by small stone borders. There is also an agricultural machinery station where the peasants can rent what they need for their plots, and a relatively frequent distribution of seeds ends the list of benefits given by the government. Yet, in this area, many heads of families with the usufruct of land declare that, if the law allowed it, they would sell their plots. Many do not work the land themselves but come to an arrangement with *isleños*—immigrant peasants from the Canaries— whereby they sow and harvest the corn for them in exchange for permission to grow a crop of potatoes for themselves at another period of the year. Most of the tenants are irregular in paying the minimal rent for their houses; and when action is threatened, a politician can always be found who will wipe out or reduce the debt, or provoke a stay of execution. For the peasants are electors and it is wise to come to terms with them.

Should one, then, accept the verdict of the Europeans who

have worked hard on this same land and created modern farms: 'They are lazy'? It is a summary judgement. The European who has come to settle here has behind him scores of generations of peasants. The man who was born here has only a tradition of gathering and harvesting. In the best of cases, he has behind him the painful experience of having been exploited on a *hacienda*. If he is ambitious, he turns towards the openings offered by the town—unless, that is, the political advantages he gains by remaining outweigh those he could derive from a difficult harvest.

Comparison with the life, methods and habits of the countries that were industrialised long ago frequently leads to moral condemnation. What is frequently overlooked is that moral attitudes are themselves the product of many factors. The tenants of the large residential blocks built by the dictator Pérez Jiménez to replace the *choza* villages he had bulldozed into the ground, are frequently described with contempt. When the *caudillo* fell, these families abandoned their modern quarters and rebuilt their corrugated iron, wood and cardboard villages. For my part, I confess that, having visited these famous 'blocks', where noise, overcrowding, smells, quarrels and the rule of the strongest remind one of prisons or barracks, I can understand perfectly well that a man who has come in from the country should prefer virtually to camp out in the open air rather than suffocate in dwellings that only veterans of Aubervilliers or the East End would find habitable.

Once again, it has not been the development of possibilities which have arisen within an evolving society, or the growth in power and influence of ambitious social groups, which modify the given factors of regional or national problems. It has been sudden disturbances, the discovery or rediscovery of Eldorados which can now be developed by modern techniques, which have placed whole populations in unprecedented situations, in dealing with which they have no experience or tradition to turn to as a guide.

178

The region of La Guayana furnishes a startling example. In 1532, Don Diego de Ordaz went up the banks of the Orinoco and founded Santo Tomé de los Guayanos. At the time, this was no more than an Indian village, and was accessible only to hardened soldiers. Even the missionaries would not go there. The site, at the junction of the Caroni with the Orinoco, was well chosen. Four centuries later the mining companies built wharfs there for loading iron ore. Between the original Santo Tomé and today's Puerto Ordaz the town died and was born again many times. In 1591, another expedition founded a new Santo Tomé, or Santo Tomás, 20 kilometres from the mouth of the Caroni. In 1619, the town was reborn, with a small garrison of forty soldiers. To natural obstacles, the hostility of the Indians and the difficulty of the climate, were added the rivalries among European powers eager for conquests. Sir Walter Raleigh's men were there around 1618 and later; the Dutch intervened between 1631 and 1679; the French came in 1685, and the English returned in 1790. When the town was refounded a fourth time, the choice of site was determined by military considerations. So as to put pirate ships within range of their cannons, the Spanish preferred the place where the Orinoco becomes narrower. This became Angostura, later called Ciudad Bolívar in honour of the liberator who was elected president there in 1819. Since then it has not been necessary to rebuild the town, but now, after the impetus given by industry in the region, we have to speak of a completely new Ciudad Bolívar and of a Santo Tomás de Guayana which will soon, in a few years' time, resemble the neighbouring centres of San Félix, Puerto Ordaz and Ciudad Bolívar.

The Indian fishermen still come in their long and unstable canoes to sell river-fish a stone's throw away from the long promenade at the edge of the town. Under the arcades, Syrian, Palestinian and Lebanese shopkeepers sell cotton clothes, hammocks and plastic crockery. The roads are filled with men dressed in white, wearing sandals and wide-brimmed

179

straw hats. There are still the façades of sumptuous consular residences (Liverpool, New Orleans, Rotterdam), and the small cemetery once reserved for non-Catholics bears witness to the number and power of the Lutherans from Lübeck, Bremen and Hamburg in the nineteenth century.

This has been the scene of many adventures, evasions, illusions, successes and disasters: gold and diamond rushes, butterfly-hunts or the collection of medicinal herbs, saps and resins. But the Orinoco does not stop and its international waters (Colombian, Brazilian and Venezuelan) flow through seventeen branches towards the Atlantic and the ports of the world. Pirate ships, paddle-boats, smoky steamers and now ore-transports have carried the feathers of rare birds, precious stones, leather and rubber; today they carry millions of tons of iron and steel ingots; tomorrow, thanks to the harnessed energy of the waters, it will be bauxite and aluminium. La Guayana, with its dreams and its dangers, is still there and the river still discharges its 18,000 tons of water every second. But the men are no longer content with simple gathering, with individual prospecting and their four stakes covered with a roof of branches. Many are returning with bulldozers, excavators and mechanical shovels, and are holding back the forest. Mining enterprises with modern equipment, processing factories, an iron and steel industry, hydroelectric dams and factories are replacing squatters' camps. In a few years, the region's capital will have several hundred thousand inhabitants, thanks to the water and to the mines, just as Maracaibo, at the other end of the country, now has half a million inhabitants thanks to oil.

Now it is the Venezuelans' turn to dream.

8. *Mexico: 'El Señor Presidente'*

The frescoes of Diego Rivera face everyone who climbs the monumental steps of the presidential palace. Amid the confusion of an outline of history, one can see hideous Spanish *conquistadores*, inquisitors with pointed cowls, a Karl Marx powerful as the Almighty Father, capitalists with their big cigars, the patriot-priest Hidalgo, the anarchist Flores Magón and the peasant war-leaders. They continue to lend their tone to the Mexican political idiom, and their inspiration was laid claim to by the former president, Adolfo López Mateos, just as it is by the present president, Gustavo Díaz Ordaz. No one is excluded from the pantheon of national heroes. It does not matter whether he belongs to the time of the Indian struggles against Cortés or whether he was born more recently, at the time of independence or of the struggles for land and freedom. From one end to the other of the vast city, there are alternate statues of Cuauhtemoc, Morelos, Juárez and Emiliano Zapata to bear witness to the continuity of a history which the Partido Revolucionario Institucional claims to have inherited and to be perpetuating.

There are, of course, other constant features of the country's tradition: the Indian population, the Church, or the de facto power which is exercised in the interior. But these, whatever their importance in the life of the country, have no right to theoretical recognition. The government knows that they exist. It takes account of them and carries out an extremely flexible policy with regard to them. But it takes steps to avoid giving them publicity proportional to their importance. The press is wary of saying too much about them, except indirectly. There is an entire history and a whole corpus of institutions which merit the permanent attention of the authorities and which are their exclusive property. Everything which does not have administrative existence continues to live and to weigh down on the country's future, but without appearing in the official transactions and chronicles of the United States of Mexico. In this respect, the government is in effect carrying on a revolutionary tradition.

The accumulation of works carried out by the régime slowly, though in some fields rapidly, changes the contrasting, chaotic and closed-in appearance of the country. Initiatives come from above and are deliberately entrusted to a single man who enjoys full power for a period of six years. 'El Señor Presidente', during the entire period of his mandate, is not subjected to any criticism. He is a true sovereign and his power is limited only by time, the rule of non-reëligibility, and the interplay of economic and international factors. In 1964, in the last few months of his mandate, the retiring president unveiled several hundred public works—buildings, dams, schools, airports, bridges and high-ways—to bear witness to his six-year period of office. In turn, his successor has sought to give impulse and orientation to the life of the country; to create and to bequeath.

The great stability of the régime—of which Mexicans are particularly proud—cannot be explained by any precise social or political formula. It is the result of a subtle policy carried out by the official party and of a special relationship between the administration and the party. In theory, they are separate; but, in fact, they are frequently interchangeable. Waves of discontent and social tensions are dampened and absorbed by the régime itself, which is skilled in personalising opposition and then in capturing and 'digesting' its representatives.

There seem to be two circuits in operation. One is established between the various sectors which can satisfy their needs only through the intervention of the state and the local party representatives with direct links with the state administration. This circuit operates above all at election time, when it becomes necessary to give the new president a certificate qualifying him to receive every complaint and to be the natural outlet for all demands. The other circuit is a permanent one, and is that which exists between the administration and the various pressure groups. In this second case, the flow of exchange between the possibilities of the former and the needs of the latter —within the limits set by the orientation which the president gives to his administration—is constant. In effect, the absolute power of the president, never questioned by the press or any other interest-group, and the infinitely varied mosaic of appetites, vested interests and new needs, become complementary aspects of the same consensual game. Each partner, the organiser included, knows how far he can go without threatening the functioning of the system.

The example of the trade-union movement is relevant here. There are many rival workers' and peasants' federations. Old federations die and new ones come into being. All, however, in the last analysis, depend on the president, whose authority and material resources are decisive. Internecine struggles, conflicts between rival clans and rebellions at the base increase the president's power of arbitrage. Not only does the movement exert no pressures on the central power, but it is even used as an instrument to control private enterprises which otherwise would not respect the unwritten laws and might express a desire to disregard the supreme will.

As for the minority political parties—Acción Nacional, Partido Socialista Popular, Movimiento de Liberación Nacional —whether they be right-wing supporters of private enterprise or belong to the extreme left, they are of any account only in so far as the Partido Revolucionario Institucional (PRI) tolerates them, gives them a secondary rôle, or uses them as an index of discontent. When the election period is opened, there is a marked disparity between the means at the disposal of the PRI and the state to promote the official candidate, and those of the marginal organisations. The mass organisations are kept under control by leaders who know that their own strength is minimal when compared with that of the régime. Directly or indirectly, every social, political, commercial and cultural activity is dependent on the state. It is true that the personnel of government, which was once purely political, is changing its composition according as new problems demand specialised solutions, and the *técnico* is beginning to play an important rôle. But he is not yet able to intervene, for the machine was devised, before his appearance on the scene, for the exclusive benefit of the *político*.

As soon as a region or a social stratum attempts to escape from the general political mechanisms, the state is in a position to control it or to bring it back into line by bringing into play the allocation of credit, administrative decrees and official authorisations. The federated states in the Union are autonomous so far as their own problems are concerned, but they cannot go it alone, since they are to a large extent dependent on the federal budget, and their leaders are solidary with the official party. Conversely, the federal government is not pleased by local governors who are unable to make themselves respected by public opinion, even if they claim allegiance to the PRI; and it has been known for governors, under pressure from student demonstrations or the protests of the business community, to be replaced by another member of the PRI.

The equilibrium of the régime is thus ensured by the certainty of the active and ambitious that they will be able to profit from the constant mobility of public offices, to participate in the game of the authorisations, favours and credits dispensed by the state: the sole proprietor and entrepreneur. Even the new bourgeoisie can accumulate capital only through the advances of money and the orders of the official organisations. It remains dependent.

This social stability, which has become one of the main elements in Mexican propaganda abroad, has provoked a considerable influx of Latin American capital, since the conditions imposed by European banking centres are no longer attractive. Exact figures belong to the vast area of taboo topics, but there is probably an excess of available finance in Mexico, and one witnesses the re-export of capital to Latin American countries. Mexico is thus in a position to become a banker. This is but one more paradoxical aspect of its revolutionary tradition.

As for the social problems which everywhere else in the continent would produce strikes, struggles and military coups: they are many, evident and serious in Mexico; but they are not explosive. Permanent unemployment can be seen in most urban centres. Even in Mexico City, fixed employment is a near-privilege. Hundreds of thousands of men and women live off precarious seasonal or occasional work. Many 'tradesmen' have no more funds than a wooden or cardboard box. Wages, despite social legislation and decrees fixing a minimum level, are generally low. At least a third of the urban workers receive less than the equivalent of £18 or $43 a month. Conditions are manifestly worse in the rural areas. On the other hand, a frontier separates the manual worker from the white-collar worker. The graduate, the intellectual, the medium- or high-grade civil servant is comfortably off. One can speak not only of two styles of life, but also of two styles of food, the poor being content with traditional foods like maize, beans and peppers, whereas the rich eat meat and dairy products. A quarter of the federal budget is devoted to education. Vast and stubborn efforts are directed to it, but in 1963 more than 2 million children were without schools. The agrarian reform marks time and the government is divided as regards giving priority to immediate or long-term objectives, as regards maintaining the *ejido* system—communal ownership, family cultivation, collective buying and selling—which has a solid bureaucracy behind it, or developing individual smallholdings.

And yet Mexico goes forward and its rate of economic growth —6 per cent annually—is impressive. Its infrastructure— energy, transports—is developing rapidly. But this impulse does not provoke any essential modification in social structure or reduce class differentials. A study of Mexican society in class terms is still lacking. Such an analysis should begin with the real significance of the university: an impressive group of modern buildings covered with avant-garde symbols and glorification of revolutionary continuity. It provides the ruling class with its most prized asset: the *licenciado*, the man who has a degree and who therefore has the right of access to power.

VI

Some Hypotheses

Having explored the varied, compartmented and stratified, but changing and largely uncatalogued societies of Latin America, we must now attempt some form of classification and try to pinpoint some of the key problems. The preceding chapters were intended to put the reader on his guard against the dangerous tendency of attempting to understand Latin America by establishing parallels with American or European experiences. In Latin America, most situations and most social and political mechanisms are *sui generis*. What must now be done is to state the main problems and to put forward a few hypotheses.

In the first place, and without thereby making any judgement as to their beneficial or harmful effects, it must be said that most of the forces of change are imported ones. Generally speaking it has not been as a result of endogenous changes linked to a natural evolution that the societies of Latin America have since the beginning of the nineteenth century been undergoing transformations and suffering disruptions. The invitations, the encouragements and the orders have come from outside.

Had it not been for the sudden irruption of the outside world in all its manifestations, the economic and social structures of Latin America would almost certainly have remained paralysed. But changes, and even profound disruptions, introduced as a result of external influences in, for example, an economic sector do not automatically imply changes in the nature of power or in the functioning of the internal systems of social relationships and mechanisms of dependence. Usually, the ruling groups of a country are not removed, or ruined, or replaced by the introduction of new techniques or by the development of productive activities that destroy the previously existing commercial equilibrium.

Indeed, it would not be hazardous to say that the forms of traditional power, the attitudes and the behaviour of the privileged groups, remain as they were, despite changes that have taken place in the economy, the public services and political administration. The psychological characteristics of the old Spanish élite survive in the ruling groups. They correspond to an admired ideal, no matter what the nature of the organisations or the men who are ruled.

This permanence of a form of power with deep roots in tradition, expert in the art of flexible self-defence, with a great capacity for absorbing and assimilating those who succeed in carving out for themselves new fiefs, explains the absence of a true peasant or industrial entrepreneurial bourgeoisie.

Capital, techniques, skilled manpower and initiatives come, most frequently, from abroad and produce changes that can be seen either as a threat or as a new hope. Opinions are seldom expressed with regard to the nation taken as a whole, but in terms of their possible short-term beneficiaries or victims. Even today, and although Latin American societies have become differentiated into a large number of heterogeneous sectors, there still exists an instinctive mistrust of any modifications in vested interests: modifications which are naturally attributed to foreign inspiration.

The case of Argentina deserves special attention in view of the fact that massive immigration was sought and organised, particularly between 1880 and 1930, by the ruling groups. They hoped to 'people the desert' and create a nation by importing from Europe everything that they thought necessary for building a modern state: manpower, capital, techniques, means of transport and educational methods. This was an original attempt, willed by an essentially urban property-owning class and conceived in rationalist terms, to replace the underpopulated, interbred traditional society, moulded by the forms of Spanish colonialism, by a nation European in form and content, by a modern state. For many reasons, the results did no correspond to the original goals. An important factor was that there existed a large gap between the liberal ideas and the actual social behaviour of the rulers of Buenos Aires. The system of parliamentary democracy was reserved for those who were of Argentine stock. It functioned, in effect, for the benefit of the large land-owning families. The mass of the immigrant population remained marginal to political life and could not become integrated in it. The 'democratisation' of agricultural property did not take place, even though in theory the immigrant labour-force had been intended for agriculture and cattle-rearing.

Gino Germani, who has published two masterly studies of the phenomenon,[1] points out that 'the traditional families had succeeded in maintaining and even increasing the preponderance of the régime of the *latifundio*. Even so late as 1947, two-thirds of the land was concentrated in a little over 20,000 landholdings, less than 6 per cent of the total number of holdings.'[2]

Only after 1930, and by methods which had nothing democratic about them, did Argentina 'Argentinise'; only then did the sons of immigrants, workers and commercial employers, bourgeois and industrialists, come into public life. The wave of foreign immigration came brusquely to an end and was replaced by internal migrations. Peronism was not far off.

A certain form of nationalism takes the form of xenophobia. It is not artificially induced, but finds expression in the popular reaction against the *Turco*, the Jew, the Italian, the *gachupino* or the *gringo*—not simply because their habits and ways of going about things are different, but because they disturb the simplified image of social relationships. Change has a foreign-looking face.

Socially, the cleavage as regards the acceptance or the rejection of what is new and imported takes place between the beneficiaries of the old order (or, more simply, those who are integrated) and the marginal, non-participant 'availables'. These reactions take place at each phase of development. The Chilean copper miner acts as a 'conservative' in so far as he is paid by an American mining company and continues to think as a 'revolutionary' as regards the government of his own country, without this preventing him from being, and from feeling himself to be, part of the system. The Argentine student is a political extremist as far as demands addressed to the Ministry of Education are concerned; once he has graduated, he goes to the US consulate in the hope of finding a job in the 'imperialist hell'.

One can well imagine the variety of long- and short-term interests that can be grouped together in anti-imperialist campaigns or nationalist movements. The socialist or radical bank clerk opposes the nationalisation of the banking system that is demanded or provoked by the competition of international credit organisations, and he will do it in the name of the national interest. On the other hand, the young technician who leaves school and finds all his roads blocked by bureaucratic proliferations will demand the reorganisation of institutions in the name of national development, even if it works so as to answer the requirements of European or American financial organisations.

The ambiguity of all social and political struggles is revealed in this double tug of 'conservative' and 'progressive'. On the one hand, there is the desire to preserve which is expressed by the traditional privileged groups who rely on all possible means of preserving the status quo, even if they belong to the middle classes or to the proletariat, and will not admit the introduction of new methods or activities except in so far as they do not threaten their over-all control. On the other hand, there is the desire for change which is expressed by the social groups who are excluded from the functioning of the traditional system and by the candidates for power.

Most of the political parties are shot through with the contradictions of this double tendency in which they necessarily have a rôle to play. Their electoral power is based on the categories of electors who are anxious to remain integrated or to become integrated in society as it exists. Their future depends on the evolution of this same society but they cannot ally themselves with any authentic forces of change. The impasse is evident and calls for the creation of a movement which would make change a national issue, which could make use of the nationalist and anti-imperialist tendencies without at the same time becoming involved in the defence of the traditional structures. In many regions of Latin America, we can see the organisation, the articulation and the launching of such movements.

When one examines individual parties, therefore, one must bear in mind that anti-imperialist and anti-capitalist attitudes do not necessarily reflect a desire for progress or even for change. Although the traditional power-groups are neither willing nor able to face the challenges put to them by the evolution of the outside world and its fatal consequences for the activities of national societies, no social class puts itself forward as a replacement. Neither the industrial bourgeoisie, nor the peasantry, nor the proletariat is a candidate for the succession. Numerically feeble, in comparison with the unstructured mass of the population, and occupying marginal or secondary positions in the economy as a whole, these classes can perform the rôle of pressure groups, but, except very rarely, they do not express a desire to rule or an *égoisme sacré*.

Since the imperatives of change exert an irresistible pressure on the decadent forms of the old structure, and since the class social-groups 'with a historic mission' cannot measure up to the problems of change and revolution, one must conclude that a new class must arise to perform this necessary function.

It is frequently said that the Latin American middle classes are acquiring an ever greater influence, and that these are the classes which must give a direction to the evolution of these changing societies and provide the answers to the new needs. Observation of these middle classes leads one to conclude that they do not constitute a class in the true sense of the term, but a fluid amalgam of infinitely varied composition. One can only say, then, that it is from this melting-pot of classes, this reservoir of socially unattached individuals, that the elements of a new ruling class may possibly emerge.

According as the needs of modernity become more pressing, as new social strata come into being, as activities in harmony with the twentieth century develop, as contacts with the outside world multiply, the need to create administrations, to make public services work and to take account of the existence and the demands of categories of citizens who cannot find a place in the relatively simple structures of post-colonial society, requires that the state, which had previously performed the rôles of policeman, soldier, magistrate and tax-collector, should grow and become more powerful.

The oligarchy is careful to keep a firm control on the services that no longer apply to its area of society, but it must also give ever more complex and essential tasks to categories of men who are no longer under its direct control and who no longer 'belong' to it as intimately and clearly as did its *peones* and servants. When new activities and functions become necessary, it is naturally the state—since there exists no other dynamic class—which performs them, whether of its own accord or at the instance of the oligarchy, or, finally, in answer to the demands of the new categories of citizens who are marginal to the old system. The state becomes progressively the site and instrument of all needs and initiatives; even when it does not possess the right of decision, the means of power are concentrated in its hands.

The long and rich social and political history of the Latin American countries in the still unfinished period of the decadence of the oligarchy provides countless examples of an original phenomenon. It is the state which benefits from most of the transfers of power, property and initiatives, to a far greater extent than do the interest-groups which are taking part in the creation of a new society.

This tendency can be explained by a number of factors, three of which seem to be decisive. In the first place, the oligarchy tends to hand over to the state, rather than to social groups which could then become its rivals, all the tasks for which it feels itself to be unsuited or ill-equipped. Secondly, the new social sectors turn to the state for the arbitration of conflicts and the safeguarding of particular rights, for the state is the legal possessor of the resources which can be exploited only by means of modern techniques. Thirdly, foreign companies and countries have accentuated the trend towards concentration by turning to the state as the entity responsible for endorsing their contracts and seeing that their agreements are kept.

The many functions of a state which is both instrument and initiator, the scene of the struggles between the traditional holders of power and new economic activities, and the meeting-place for all confrontations, not only explain the contradictions and paradoxes of this indefinable monster; they also cause the state to grow and to employ a high proportion of the active population. The state is becoming a society.

In the administrations, the services and the state-controlled enterprises, the theoretical anonymity of the public organisations exists only on paper. In fact, the hundreds of thousands of state employees depend on the state budget for their pay-slips. But they are also dependent on the party in power, on opposition parties, on an autonomous public sector, or on private groups whose economic activities are closely linked to the goodwill of a ministerial department. In many countries in the sub-continent, it is openly admitted that a civil servant or even a statesman can combine public functions and private activities.

One of the most worrying situations is that of the armed forces. For a long time they constituted the backbone of the state. In many countries, they are still the only well-articulated organisation which can of its own accord replace any civil government. In others, they can exercise the right of veto against a form of government or a policy which they think goes against the national interest or jeopardises their own existence. An exceptional case is the Paraguayan one, where the army controls the party in power, and not vice-versa. Where the army occupies the presidential palace, the tendency is to give the levers of command to civilians, subject to certain restrictions. And these restrictions amount to the maintenance of the status quo in the political struggle or to ensuring the non-revolutionary nature of changes.

The army does not, in fact, have the organisation with which to control the country. It can govern but it cannot administer, except with difficulty and for a limited period of time. It must, therefore, come to terms with the civil powers. The choice of these powers is, however, determined by the consideration that no military-civilian alliance is possible which would deprive the army of its rôle as arbiter of power.

This opposition between the army, as a 'power factor' in the strict sense of the term, conscious of its limitations as a driving force for society (even though there is sometimes a tendency for the army to take on the functions of a political party), and a potential new ruling class cannot thus be explained in terms of social origins or conflicts in policy. The opposition derives from the simple fact that the army and the new ruling class are two political formulas which are by definition mutually exclusive.

The stakes in the struggle for power are far more than simply the control of the ministerial administrations and a say in general policy-making. Access to power, by parliamentary or by more direct means, in many Latin American countries implies the availability of the sizeable and decisive resources of the state, recourse to the public revenue (which frequently represents a considerable proportion of the national income) and the possibility of innovation in the field of industrialisation. The influence wielded by a pressure-group, the weight of a political party or the audience obtainable by means of agitation or propaganda bear no comparison with the possibilities offered by the use of the state's power. This, rather than the psychological factors frequently adduced by outside observers, is the real explanation of the violence and bitterness of political struggles in Latin America. The resources of power sharpen appetites and ambitions. This is true regardless of whether they are oriented towards personal gain, those of one's clan or *clientela*, or the transformation of society.

The new political class, which one can observe coming into being and whose members are present wherever institutions or organisations to deal with the problems of development are being created, is made up of non-producers. Its members belong essentially to the managerial, technical and organisational strata. This tertiary sector exists, of course, in the industrialised countries as well, but what makes it a class in itself in Latin America are its rôle as an agent of change, its dominant position within the state, and its clearly expressed political will to control the state, to *be* the state.

In the various Latin American régimes of today, some pre-some post-revolutionary, one is struck by the degree to which the main rôle in bringing about change is performed by intellectuals and 'organisers', and also by the degree to which the most direct and numerous beneficiaries of this change are the same intellectuals and 'organisers'. The holders of top positions in the parties which are candidates for power

—be they Marxist, Socialist or Christian Democrat—are strangely alike, particularly as regards their social origins.

The frequently violent struggles fought by opposition parties and factions should not be allowed to obscure what is common to them in class terms: their social function and their consciousness of that function. Nor should the vicissitudes of change and the particular conditions of each situation lead one to neglect the more general aspects of the phenomenon.

The main internal contradiction of the new class, born of the difference between the intellectuals—experts in the political game and in the struggle for power—and the technically oriented professionals, cannot become evident until this class has obtained power. The rôle of the former is clearly more important in the conquest of power, and the formation of a political apparatus can hamper the normal functioning of the activities of the latter, particularly if international factors arise to exacerbate internal rivalries.

A further error of interpretation can arise from the superficial oppositions that divide related groups in a situation of change. Between the white-collar establishment and similar groups with no chances of mobility, there is a rivalry but no fundamental difference.

The large number of 'availables', augmented by each passing generation and frustrated by the narrowness of possibilities, is tempted to engage in political struggles in order to achieve power or at any rate to approach the sources of power. Even those who have non-political means at their disposal for making a career or for participating in economic activities—professionals, graduates, white-collar workers, 'superannuated' students and trade-union militants—soon find that the major decisions are taken by those who dispose of power and that they cannot despise the decisive rôle of the state.

The external appearance of partisan struggles, factional polemics, the sometimes Ubuesque flavour of propaganda campaigns or the pomposity of manifestos, should not lead one to forget what is central: the sudden *prise de conscience* of a new class and the search for a means of taking over or participating in power. The vocabularies which clothe these efforts and the apparent versatility of the leaders of political factions cannot conceal the importance of the process that is under way.

Ideology, even when formulated, is generally speaking only the presentation of a means of obtaining power. What really interests most of the leaders and activists of reformist or revolutionary groups are ways and means. Hence the large number of borrowings from doctrines or methods which seem to have triumphed in other places and circumstances; hence, too, the rapidity with which the militants of these groups change their theoretical justifications or foreign models.

Within the last few years, such 'models' have succeeded one another with astonishing speed, without any change having taken place in the fundamental goals. We have now reached the stage where analyses of national situations are replacing transplants and adaptations of foreign models. The writings of the Mexican sociologist Rodolfo Stavenhagen are significant in this respect. His study, 'Seven Mistaken Theses on Latin America',[3] is primarily directed against formulas in support of free enterprise and the 'national bourgeoisie', but at the same time it shatters a number of so-called revolutionary clichés, such as 'the alliance between workers and peasants'.

This new phase is of crucial importance. It means that the period of imitation, which was in effect a form of escapism, is over and that the rôle of technicians—of both theory and action—will from now on be essential. Although 'Che' Guevara's little book[4] has been taken as a manual for those who aspire to power, a kind of storehouse of revolutionary know-how, and although, fifteen days before the Algerian leader was displaced by Boumedienne, a Peruvian guerrilla leader could choose 'Ben Bella' as his *nom de guerre*, experience has finally shown that there is no single model of how to take power.

But the vocabulary remains. It takes up the European terminology of the class struggle, the leading rôle of the proletariat, the driving-force of the peasantry, the Socialist conception of tomorrow's society. But even here wear and tear has its effects. So great is the contrast between reality and the formulas which are supposed to apply to it that revision and modification become inevitable.

More recently, some representatives of national liberation movements, mainly in Africa, but in other areas of the Third World as well, have put forward the idea that, in colonial, semi-colonial and neo-colonial countries, the decisive class is the 'petty bourgeoisie'. The clearest exponent of this new theoretical approach is Amilcar Cabral, leader of the liberation movement in Portuguese Guinea. He has been followed, with some reserve, by the the experts who write for Communist magazines.[5]

This new thesis, despite dialectical acrobatics and reinterpretations of the sacred texts, no longer corresponds in any way to the classical conception of vulgar Marxism. It does, on the other hand, take account of a clear fact: the leaders of the revolutionary parties are neither workers nor peasants. It is easier to find in the ranks of the Venezuelan or Peruvian *guerrilleros* the products of the upper middle class or of the oligarchy than a single steel- or plantation-worker.

As for the term 'petty bourgeoisie' (*pequeñe burguesia*), it is at least as ambiguous as 'middle classes', which it appears to want to replace. So great is the ambiguity that Cabral has to take his argument further and declare that this 'petty bourgeoisie' will have to choose between its bourgeois destiny and its transformation, by 'suicide', into the servant and guide of the poorer classes. This way of approaching the problem, unorthodox for a social scientist whatever the school he follows, amounts to admitting the impossibility of defining, by reference to previously classified classes, what he calls the 'petty bourgeoisie', whose future is not clear. A definition becomes possible if one is prepared to admit the coming into being of a new class, whose boundaries, content and social function are much clearer than those of the 'petty bourgeoisie'.

Other theoretical approximations will doubtless follow and attempt to reconcile what can be seen and the terms used to define it. These efforts will continually come up against the fixed tradition of revolutionary language which has been in use for over a century. This task of clarification will be all the more difficult since the new ruling class cannot hope to gain power unless it has the support or active participation of the workers and peasants, and consequently a certain degree of imprecision will be necessary.

The proletariat obviously has an interest in knowing what are the views of those who make up the new ruling class in regard to the rôle and the rights of the workers and peasants, and the opinion of them that is implicit in these views. This is no more than a pious hope, and it will remain one so long as independent organisations do not express the way of life, the hopes and the ways of thinking of manual workers.

Here we touch on another phenomenon which is peculiar to, or particularly acute in, the countries of Latin America: namely, the absence of a solid network of grass-roots organisations which could represent the workers and the peasants, reflecting the desire of the citizen to participate from the base and to deal with the problems for which he is equipped. Unions, peasant leagues, co-operatives, mutual-benefit societies and neighbourhood organisations are, where they exist, mere branches of political parties or dependent on the public administration. Social and labour legislation, which is frequently 'advanced'—on paper—encloses the wage-earners in a narrow straitjacket of regulations which limits their every possibility of manoeuvre and initiative. Most industrial conflicts reflect this fact; they are not so much a direct struggle with the employer as an attempt to induce the state to intervene. This situation, in which the worker or the peasant has no means of action under his own control, does not seem to worry the spokesmen of the new class, even when they claim to represent realism and popular revolution.

Although the modern parties grasp the theoretical importance of real, responsible and conscious participation on the part of the workers' or peasants' organisations, all their efforts are naturally directed towards the construction of machines with which to seize power, not towards the slow and difficult task of creating associations in the workplaces and neighbourhoods.

Under these conditions, however great the goodwill and good faith of the new class's political leaders, there is a strong temptation to continue to manipulate the labour-force as a statistical datum on a par with raw materials. One should clearly not underestimate the important difference between totalitarian methods of control, with a single party and naked coercion, and procedures which at least assure the individual of his self-defence and a possibility of refusal. But what must equally be understood is that, for all that the choice of method depends on the government's intentions, it depends still more on the active existence of organisations which can perform a countervailing rôle and restrain possible abuses of power. It would be foolish to believe that the moral principles which originally inspire the new holders of state power will be able to resist the exhilarations of power, the taste for rapid and spectacular public works, and the all too easy confusion between public power and the welfare of the citizens.

Paradoxically, if one is to believe the Socialist and communitarian language of the new parties, their desired goals correspond to the achievements of the régimes which they condemn in the strongest terms: the Soviet Union and the United States. Change and progress are everywhere in Latin America conceived of as an attempt to catch up as quickly as possible with the highly industrial societies. One may be permitted a certain scepticism as to how easily this transformation can be brought about, even by totalitarian means. One may even express some doubts as to the type of industrial society which has been chosen. It is admittedly attractive for those who know only the archaic, unjust and unegalitarian societies of Latin America, but its ideal character is only relative. There is a danger that the only things that may remain after such imitation are the worst techniques of wielding power.

'Socialism' and 'Community' correspond to a view of society in which the totality of human and material resources is mobilised for the common good. The lack of precision is deliberate, for the functioning of such a society and the fact that it must have rulers present problems which immediately shatter the idyllic image of 'Socialism' or 'Community'. What is common to the two terms is the wishing away of conflict for the benefit of a collectivity whose harmony— although this is not clearly expressed—would derive from the wisdom and foresight of its rulers. 'Socialism' or 'Community' is born of a will from above and is not the result of a series of experiences in which the workers' associations would take part and finally take over, as the original Socialists had hoped.

One would hope that at least the Europeans and North Americans who are so prodigal in recipes they have not tried out would be prudent in their offer of magic solutions, even if they are afraid of being overtaken by a revolution. Too much emphasis on economic indices and figures which measure economic expansion frequently leads experts and planners to forget what human suffering is. Without suspecting it, they form part of a technocratic tradition. For their sake, it seems appropriate to end with two quotations from the same work which can serve as a warning against generous, and scientific, intentions whose results are sometimes catastrophic. They are the proposals made by M. Michel Chevalier, a member of the

Institut and follower of Saint-Simon, at the beginning of Napoleon III's Mexican campaign in 1862.

Thanks to the prompt and economical means of communication offered by modern civilisation, large-scale migrations become easy. We have just seen that hundreds of thousands of people made the journey to the United States every year, until they were decimated by the Civil War. It would be as easy to people Mexico with Chinese immigrants as it has been to people the Mississippi Valley or the upper basin of the St Lawrence with the children of Ireland or farmers from the banks of the Rhine or the Oder. . . .

The most formidable adversary which our valiant soldiers have had to face on their journey is the yellow fever. But although this disease is formidable, it ceases to rage at a short distance from the river. To fight this scourge the government has decided to use two means simultaneously, each efficient in its own way. The first is the construction of a railroad by means of which the troops, no sooner disembarked at Vera Cruz, could cross in a few hours the infected area and be taken to Orizaba, where they could breathe perfectly pure air. The other is to employ Negro soldiers to occupy Vera Cruz and its citadel, the castle of San Ulua. One could take them from our nearby colonies, Martinique and Guadeloupe, and one could borrow them from the viceroy of Egypt, for whom it would be an honour to mix his troops with those of France. It is well-known that members of the Negro race have the privilege of being able to face contagion with impunity, as they do the burning rays of the equatorial sun. Spain had often thought of stationing Negro troops in Vera Cruz. But given the rusty mechanisms of that government, any form of progress was difficult and this humane idea was never put into execution.[6]

References

I CLASSES

1. F. Bourricaud, "La Oligarquía en el Perú", *Eco*, Bogotá, November 1965.
2. Ibid.
3. Elisée Reclus, *Mis exploraciones en América*, F. Sempera, Valencia 1861.
4. E. R. Wolf, *Sons of the Shaking Earth*, University of Chicago Press, Chicago 1959, p. 230.
5. Ibid., p. 205.
6. Much in our discussion of the Brazilian situation is derived from Benno Galjart, "Class and 'Following' in Rural Brazil", *América Latina*, VII, 3, 1964. Galjart eschews the intellectual romanticism that tends to characterise much that is written about north-east Brazil.
7. Aníbal Pinto Santa Cruz, *Chile: Un Caso de desarrollo frustrado*, Editorial Universitaria, Santiago 1958.
8. José Luis de Imaz, *Los que mandan*, Eubeda, Buenos Aires 1964.
9. Aaron Lipman, "Social Background of the Bogotá Entrepreneur", *Journal of Inter-American Studies*, 1965, p. 231.
10. Theodore Geiger, preface to Frank Brandenburg, *The Development of Latin American Private Enterprise*, National Planning Association, Washington D.C. 1964.
11. Brandenburg, op. cit.
12. Albert Lauterbach, "Government and Development: Managerial Attitudes in Latin America", *Journal of Inter-American Studies*, 1965, p. 22.
13. Fernando Henrique Cardoso, "The Industrial Elite", in S. M. Lipset and A. Solari (eds), *Elites in Latin America*, Oxford University Press, London 1967, p. 100.
14. Ibid., p. 102.

II CHALLENGES AND GAMBLES

1. Kingsley Davis, "La situación de América Latina en la história demográfica mundial", *América Latina*, 1964.

References

2. Ibid.
3. J. F. de Camargo, *Demográfia económica*. Livrarria Progresso, Bahia 1960.
4. Raúl Sosa Rodríguez, *Les Problèmes structurels des relations économiques internationales de l'Amérique Latine*, Librairie Droz, Geneva 1963.
5. Carlos L. Yegros Doria, in *Universidad y Estudiantes*, Ed. Liberia, Buenos Aires 1965.
6. J. L. de Imaz, *Los que mandan*, op. cit.
7. Brandenburg, *The Development of Latin American Private Enterprise*, op. cit.
8. Pablo González Casanova, *La Democracia en México*, Ed. Era, Mexico City 1965.
9. Víctor Urquidi, *Viabilidad económica de América latina*, Fondo de Cultura Económica, Mexico City 1962.
10. Raymond Vernon, *The Dilemma of Mexico's Development*, Harvard University Press, Cambridge, Mass. 1963.

III THEORIES OF THE NEW POWER

1. Helio Jaguaribe, *Burguesia y proletariado en el nacionalismo brasileño*, Ed. Coyoacán, Buenos Aires 1961.
2. Cf. "Semanas sociales de Chile", *La Comunidad nacional*, Ed. del Pacífico, Santiago 1964.
3. J. Silva Solar and J. Chonchol, *El Desarrollo de la nueva sociedad en América Latina*, Ed. Universitaria, Santiago 1965.
4. Torcuato di Tella, *¿Socialismo en la Argentina?*, Ed. Jorge Alvarez, Buenos Aires 1965.

IV FOREIGN PRESSURES

1. 'Espartaco', *Crítica a la Izquierda Latinoamericana*, Ed. Arca, Montevideo 1965.
2. W. S. Woytinsky, "The U.S. and Latin America's Economy", *The New Leader*, November 28, 1958.
3. Víctor Urquidi, *Viabilidad económica de América Latina*, op. cit.
4. Abundant documentation on the problem of violence in Colombia has been collected by Monsignor Germán Guzmán Campos, Orlando Fals Borda and Eduardo Umaña Luna, in *La Violencia en Colombia*, Ed. Tercer Mundo, Bogotá: Vol. I, 1962; Vol. II, 1964.

V SITUATIONS AND EXPERIENCES

1. Florestan Fernandes, mimeographed paper presented at a conference on Race and Colour, held in Copenhagen in 1965.
2. León Zafrán, in the symposium *El periodismo por dentro*, Ed. Libera, Buenos Aires 1965.
3. Aldo Solari, cited in *Marcha*, Montevideo, November 22, 1963.

4. Luis Danussi, in an interview with the author, July, 1962.
5. Riego Rivas, in an interview with the author, July, 1962.
6. Statement by Americo Ghioldi, leader of the Social Democratic party.
7. *El Mercurio*, Santiago, February 18, 1964.
8. Eduardo Frei Montalva, in an interview with the author, September 6, 1964.
9. Boris Goldenberg, *The Cuban Revolution and Latin America*, Allen and Unwin, London 1965, p. 290; Frederick A. Praeger, New York, 1965.

VI SOME HYPOTHESES

1. Gino Germani, *Política y Sociedad en una época de transición*, Ed. Paidos, Buenos Aires 1692, chs. 7 and 8.
2. Ibid., p. 221.
3. Rodolfo Stavenhagen, "Sept thèses erronées sur l'Amérique Latine", *Partisans*, Nos. 26–27, 1966.
4. Ernesto 'Che' Guevara, *La Guerra de Guerrillas*, Havana.
5. Cf. Amilcar Cabral, speech to the Tricontinental Conference held in Havana, January 1966; Rubén Iscaro, "El movimiento obrero y la lucha por la liberación de América latina", *Revista Internacional*, Prague, March 1966; Amilcar Cabral, "Los estudiantes en la revolución latinoamericana", ibid.; Luis Figueroa, "Algunos problemas del movimiento obrero en América latina", ibid.; Anwar Ramsy and Alexei Levkovski, "Las masas pequeñoburguesas y los movimientos revolucionarios del tercer mundo", *Problemas de la paz y del socialismo*, Bogotá, Vol. IX, 1, 1966.
6. Michel Chevalier, *Le Mexique, ancien et moderne*, Hachette, Paris 1863, pp. 461, 509.

Index

Index

Index